Born A Third Culture Kid

David C. Whitten

Table of Contents

My Ancestors

Like most people, I am proud of my family. I am not a self-made man. Most of what I have comes from my parents. Most of what they were came from their parents. I look so much like my father that people who have never met me, but know my father, called me "that Charles Whitten looking guy." I like hearing that. Many times in my life, I have said, something and then thought to myself, "that's my mother talking." DNA tells you a lot about your past. Upbringing predicts more about your future.

The first Whitten to immigrate to America was Thomas Whitten, who boarded the ship Elizabeth and Anne in 05/09/1635.

It's not very big. It carried around 20 passengers and crew and took weeks to cross the ocean

He left Hook Norton, Oxfordshire with his wife, Audrey Corke three stepchildren from a previous marriage of hers and a six-year-old who was born to them, Jeremy Whiton. It was an arduous trip and also cost Thomas Whitten the equivalent of one year's income.

Thomas and Audry landed in Plymouth, Massachusetts in July 1635, sixteen years after the Mayflower had arrived. Thomas and Audrey Whitten were given a certificate by their local pastor in England that they were religiously correct.

England was experiencing conflicts between the Roman Catholic church, the Anglican Church, and the Puritan Movement. My ancestors came to The US as Anglicans, but were probably not devout members of the church. Thomas and his descendants moved from Massachusetts to Maryland to Virginia and then to South Carolina.

The Whittens consolidated in South Carolina. In search of lands, some moved to Georgia and some moved to a triangular area involving counties in Pontotoc County, Mississippi, Marion County, Alabama, and Wayne County, Tennessee. This is where the modern Whitten family began. Eventually, they ended up in Northeast Mississippi.

The Founding Father Of The Modern Whitten Family

Henry Millholland Whitten was born in Pontotoc, Mississippi in 1862. His parents were Littleton Augustus Whitten and Lucinda Pearlee Whitten. Henry never knew his father. Before he was born, Littleton (age 59) enlisted in the Confederate army and died in one of the first major battles. He was not listed on any troop and wasn't listed among casualties. The family story is that he was killed at the Battle of Corinth, Mississippi and shoveled into a mass grave. Lucinda had four other children. They settled in Alabama and Mississippi. Lucinda lived with her youngest son, Henry, until her death at the age of 66 in 1894.

Henry had to drop out of school after the sixth grade. Neither Alabama nor Mississippi had the money for much public education after the Civil War. Henry had a thirst for knowledge but couldn't afford to pay for education. As soon as he could, he took jobs to support his mother.

The Whittens at the time were not churchgoers. Henry fell in love with a 22-year-old woman named Amanda Elizabeth Roebuck. Her family included several Baptist preachers. With Amanda's encouragement, Henry became a devout Christian.

After years of worshiping with Amanda, Henry felt the call to preach. It was too late for him to return to school for formal education. He collected books on preaching and read his Bible intensely. He consulted with his preacher, and the Pastor mentored him. When the church thought he was ready, they gave him a license to preach.

I call Rev. Henry M. Whitten the founding father of my Whitten family because of his long-term influence on the family, extending almost 100 years after he died. In Henry's youth, the Whittens were wanderers. After he established a family in Northeast Mississippi, they had a long-term home. With his influence, the family was solidly Baptist, committed to following Jesus Christ. Although he began with little education, he spent his life developing his knowledge and passing this knowledge to his children.

My grandfather is sitting on the stool. Taken in 1893

Rev. Henry M. Whitten pastored many churches in Choctaw and Winston counties in his 40 years of ministry. He obtained an architectural design for a church from the Jackson office of the Baptist convention and used this to help build four churches. One of those churches was Beulah Baptist, the home church of my father when he was growing up. He was invited to preach revivals.

A Revival is a long series of church services, often spanning a week or more. The local church invites a dynamic preacher to stir the congregation. In 1928, Henry preached a revival at Fentress, Mississippi. A 14-year-old called by his middle name, Pleemon, made a profession of faith and was baptized by Henry. The young man, whose full name was James Pleemon Coleman, was elected governor of Mississippi in 1955. In the early '60s, he was appointed to the Federal Fifth Circuit Court of Appeals. In 1980 he gave me a job as his law clerk, giving me a boost in my career. It can be said that almost a half-century after Rev. Henry died, he got a job for his great-grandson.

Henry and Amanda had four children, one of which was my grandfather, Willie Amzie Whitten. My grandfather enjoyed life as the son of a prominent preacher. As many preacher's sons, he had a rebellious streak. He drank alcoholic beverages, smoked and played with guns. In a careless moment, the rifle he was carrying fired accidentally, hitting himself in the jaw. Fortunately, it didn't hit his brain. He was allowed many more years to live and to develop maturity.

Willie moved to Memphis. He got a job as a trolley car driver. He looked impressive in his uniform, but after a few months of work decided this was not for him. In a prodigal son moment, he returned home and apologized to his parents.

Willie returned to Beulah church. Henry had been the pastor there. Beulah had been established in 1866 by laymen including Henry Peter Eddleman. Henry's son, John Henry Eddleman and his wife, Sarah Elizabeth Eddleman, gave birth to 13 children. One of those was

Velma Elizabeth Eddleman. Willie fell in love with Velma. They were married in 1917 and celebrated 63 anniversaries of their marriage.

After their marriage, Willie had some wild oats left. He went drinking with some friends, was arrested for public intoxication and spent a weekend in jail. Velma collected him after he served his sentence and asked him if this was to be a habit. Willie said his drinking was over. He kept his word and became a pillar of his church, first at Beulah and later at Weir Baptist church.

When Willie was growing up, he did not imagine himself as a farmer. His father was well-read and knowledgeable about current events. After his efforts to enter the world of public transportation failed, he decided to try farming. Many people in the community had farmed for generations. Willie's father was a preacher, and his grandfather had been a bricklayer. Willie almost earned the first high school diploma in the family. The story was that he didn't get his diploma from Kosciusko High School because he failed Latin class.

Willie was not sod-buster, to use a disparaging term said of farmers. He consulted the agricultural department at Mississippi State University, and they gave him experimental seed. He allowed them to investigate how the seed worked out and got more expert advice from them. Willie called his farm "Sunny Side Farm." Willie worked outside in the hot Mississippi sun, but he was no redneck.

Charles and Paul on a Model A. Velma is inside the car. Willis is taking the picture.

Other farmers in Willie's area might have turned down assistance from people with diplomas who had less experience farming than them. Willie welcomed the free seed and the free help. These savings enabled him to afford a Model A Ford sedan, a Victrola, and a large radio to listen to the popular series, Fibber McGee and Molly and the hilarious but infamous Amos and Andy.

Velma became a great mother and later grandmother. She had a better-than-average education and a deep devotion to God. She learned to play the piano in her parents' parlor. Her greatest regret in life was that she and Willie didn't have any daughters. Her first child died shortly after birth. Then she gave birth to Henry Paul Whitten (1919), Charles William Whitten (1922) and W.A. Whitten, Jr. (1929).

Paul and Charles (top row). Willie, WA Jr. and Velma, bottom row

God's First Gift To Me: Charles And Nella Dean Whitten

My parents were both raised on farms, my father in Choctaw County, and mother in Winston County, about 25 miles apart. My father was 3 months older than my mother. They had mutual friends but did not meet until they both entered the Baptist seminary in Louisville, Kentucky, in 1944.

My father, Charles William Whitten, was born near Weir, Mississippi, on September 4, 1922. There were complications in his birth, and he and my grandmother spent three weeks in the Baptist Hospital in Jackson, the state capital. The bill was over $100 and included charges of $1 for meals when my grandfather was there. It may seem ridiculously low today, but it was a large financial burden for a farmer just before harvest.

Charles had an older brother, Paul, born three years before him. Paul developed a stutter early in childhood. Willie and Velma went to a clinic in Memphis that tried controversial and ineffective ways to cure him. Despite his speech impediment, Paul was highly intelligent, like his two brothers. The youngest brother, Willie Amzie Whitten Jr., was born in 1929.

Because Velma did not have any daughters, the oldest sons had to divide domestic chores in the house as well as farm chores outside the house; when Paul broke his arm, Charles tried to show him ways to do chores, such as pumping water from a well, using only one arm. Despite Charles' demonstrations, Paul pretended not to understand.

Willie had a sly sense of humor, which was passed on to all his sons and grandchildren as well. He loved funny stories. One story was of a bitterly cold winter day. A farmhand stopped by and warmed his hands by the fire. After saying nothing for an extended period of time, he said, "Calf's in the well."

There was some slapstick humor. Paul was the slowest getting ready for church, often leaving others waiting impatiently in their car, waiting for him to come. Paul emerged from the house immaculately dressed, except that he had no pants on. His mother told him he had forgotten something. He said, "Oh yes, my Bible." He went back for it and emerged shortly, still without his pants.

Willie and Velma were devout Baptists, attending Beulah when the boys were young and later transferring to Weir Baptist Church. A beautiful table used for "Lord's Supper" ingredients at Weir Baptist Church has their name on it, showing they donated it. Charles made a profession of faith before he was a teenager and felt the call to follow his grandfather, Henry, into the ministry.

Charles developed musical talents. One of the helpers around the farm gave him a used harmonica when Charles was a toddler. With a little instruction, he became adept at playing popular songs of the day. He became so good at the harmonica at age four that he was lifted onto the stage at a local school to play a mini-concert.

Charles and Paul learned how to play the guitar.

L to R Charles, Paul and W.A.

When Paul was 16 and Charles was 13, they were invited to perform at a local radio station. Occasionally, they would ask their father to provide special effects. In a song about riding on a train, Willie was supposed to say "tickets, tickets" at a designated time. When Willie said the words, they echoed back at him, causing him to run out of the studio. The sons teased him about this for years.

Charles had a beautiful tenor voice. He would sing at parties and in church. I never tired of hearing him sing, sometimes as a duet with my mother. One of the great honors of my life was to accompany him on the piano. His all-time favorite hymn was "How Great Thou Art" by Stuart Hines.

In high school, Charles participated in the Future Farmers of America and the Woodmen of the World. Henry had worked for the latter as a side hustle. On his death, the Woodmen gave Henry a beautiful headstone. Charles received a scholarship for college from both organizations. The Woodman scholarship was usable at any college but was only a partial scholarship. The Future Farmer's scholarship gave him a full ride, but it was only usable at Mississippi State University.

Charles ended his senior year tied with another student for the highest grade point average. Paul had been the valedictorian three years earlier. They lived in a small community. The principal thought that it would suggest favoritism if the same family got this honor twice, so they broke the tie, making Charles the salutatorian. My father rarely complained about anything. This is one of the few occasions. He didn't think he had been treated fairly.

Charles considered enrolling at Mississippi State, thinking it was unwise to waste a scholarship. He had no intention of becoming a farmer and decided that accepting this scholarship would seem dishonest. Instead, he enrolled at Mississippi College in Clinton, Mississippi. It was farther from home, but it had a good reputation for training future preachers. Charles' uncle, John Whitten, Willie's older brother, had briefly enrolled at MC in 1909, also planning to enter the ministry. John developed appendicitis and died on a train ride back home.

Charles was active in student activities at MC, including in church activities at First Baptist in Clinton. He informed the pastors that he felt the calling to preach. The church took him under its wings and later ordained him to preach.

The ministerial department at MC gave Charles many opportunities to preach at small churches nearby. Charles pushed himself too hard in classes and in his preaching. After one sermon, Charles was not feeling well. One of the parishioners expressed concern about his appearance, saying he looked pale. Charles asked him how he could see this from the audience. The helpful parishioner said, "I'm an undertaker."

Charles had scarlet fever, a much more serious condition before easy access to antibiotics. He spent three weeks in the infirmary at Mississippi College. Despite this setback, Charles completed his bachelor's degree in three years. He enrolled in a Baptist seminary in Louisville, Kentucky.

Nella Dean Mitchell Whitten, my mother Nella Dean, was the firstborn child of Earlie Virgil Mitchell and Molly Marie McCully. She was born on December 8, 1922, a day before what was to be called Pearl Harbor Day. We teased my mother that the day after her birth was "a day that will live in infamy," to quote Franklin Delano Roosevelt. Her parents came from a long line of farmers.

Nella Dean had three younger siblings: Bruce (1926), Bob (1929), and Henry Cooper (always called H.C.), born in 1936. As with an only daughter, she got the lion's share of chores in the house, mostly helping her mother with cooking and taking care of her younger brothers. Nella Dean didn't like her first name. In college she was nicknamed Indy, combining her first two initials. That name stuck for the rest of her life.

Indy enjoyed reading and creative writing more than cooking and cleaning. When she was 4 years old, she learned that kids were going to a one-room schoolhouse down the road from her house. She asked if she could go too. She was told that she was too young, she was not deterred. Her parents became exhausted from telling on her no, so they dressed her up and gave her a writing notebook, letting her sit in class.

Indy noticed the other kids, who were more than two years older than her, had learned the alphabet. She resolved to learn it backward, starting at the letter Z. She didn't quit this experiment because of being academically behind but because none of the kids would interact with her. When Indy returned to school at 6, she remained precocious. In second grade, a teacher observed her tutoring other students her age and suggested that she should be moved up one grade. Indy graduated from school at 16.

Ironically, these events were recreated in her children. I started school at age five and graduated at seventeen. My brother John asked to start school at 5. He was actually a month older than when I began school. John had learned how to read before he started the first grade. When a teacher saw John teaching another student how to read, they suggested he be moved up to second grade. My mother couldn't say no to me, but she said no to John on both of his requests.

The Mitchells did not attend church regularly. At age 16, a girlfriend of my mother's invited her to Poplar Flat Baptist Church. Indy thought it was rude to refuse, so she got permission from her parents. When she asked to attend Sunday night services, Earl put his foot down. The walk to church was more than three miles down a dark, unpaved road. It would be too dangerous for an unaccompanied young woman to make this walk in the dark. Her brother, Bruce, then 11, volunteered to be his sister's bodyguard. It was a fortuitous moment for both. Indy went on to mission work, and Bruce later became a deacon in his church.

Indy was highly intelligent as well as gregarious. Her red hair made her stand out in the crowd. She became acutely aware of the unfair treatment of Black people in Mississippi and of women everywhere. As a young woman, she asked why a woman could not be president or the pastor of a church. Women had obtained the vote less than 20 years earlier. She got tired of being told this was how things were done or that it was God's will.

Not being one to beat her head against a wall, she stopped asking these questions but never stopped considering this to be unfair. I would not describe my mother as a feminist, as this term was used in the 1960s. My mother's example was the basis for my belief in equality for both genders.

One reason that my mother had to walk to church was her father had to give up his auto in the worst parts of the Great Depression. This made it more difficult for Indy to participate in social activities at school or at church. Somehow, she found a way.

When Indy graduated from high school, her brothers were 12, 9, and 2 years old. Her parents expected her to stay at home and help her mother with her younger brothers. At 16 she was just about the age to be socializing with eligible bachelors and probably to marry a farmer's son from the neighborhood.

Indy told them she would be attending Mississippi School for College Women in Columbus, Mississippi. Earl was appalled! She would not be at home to take care of her brothers. Earl and Marie already knew her to be stubborn. She would become an educated, stubborn woman. What man would want to marry a woman smarter than him? (The answer: a smart man who appreciated having a wife who was his intellectual equal. That worked for me.)

Indy enjoyed two years at MSCW. In her first few months, her finances were very low. Earl found out about it and drove to the campus, asking for financial aid for his daughter. She got enough to make it through two years but had to forgo a third year because she didn't have the money.

Indy returned to her parents' home and obtained a job teaching at a local elementary school. Some of the students had older brothers who noticed the pretty redhead teaching there. She received written requests for dates. She had already decided that she was called to mission work, so she turned down all requests. Indy saved enough money and found financial aid that enabled her to complete her degree at a women's college in Blue Mountain, Mississippi. She graduated with honors in 1944.

After being told that she was too smart to attract a husband and having rejected any local suitors because of their lack of ambition, Indy began to believe that she would be single all her life, a "spinster," as the term was used then. She had heard of missions in South America and believed that God was calling her into mission work there. Indy told her parents that she had been accepted at a women's institute for Christian work adjacent to the seminary in Louisville, Kentucky. Earl and Marie knew there was no way they could discourage her.

One maxim in my family is that when you tell God you are OK with being single in His service, He smiles and sends you a perfect candidate to marry.

When Charles Meets Indy

My parents met for the first time in Louisville, Kentucky, at a church social. Although the men and the women were segregated in their theological studies, young men still wanted to meet pretty girls, and pretty girls wanted to check out eligible bachelors. Charles and Indy each arrived with an escort of the opposite sex. In a mixer, they discovered that they were both from Northeast Mississippi. Their common interests made them talk for so long that their escorts changed partners. Charles and Indy learned that they had acquaintances in common. They also shared one common interest: the desire to serve the Lord in South American missions.

When my mother heard the Whitten name, she felt a little dread. In the early 1900s a group of Whittens in Winston County had been involved in a bloody fight that began at a wedding. The groom took as his bride a woman who had previously dated his older brother. "Dating" more than 125 years ago was more serious than it is today.

The older brother resented his brother marrying his former girlfriend. At the wedding ceremony, he became drunk and abusive and was kicked out of the celebrations.

After the ceremony, the new groom and bride thought they could placate the angry older brother. They traveled over to his property. The older brother had continued drinking and was not interested in talking to them. He warned them to stay out of his yard. When the groom and the bride's father entered his yard anyway, the older brother and his friend confronted them and ended up shooting and killing them.

The two shooters fled into the woods and hid there for more than a year. Sympathetic family members brought them food. The police decided not to challenge them. Their family members eventually tired of the effort and expense and persuaded them to come out and take their medicine. The shooters were not persuasive in their arguments of self-defense and ended up with ten-year sentences for manslaughter. They served two years and grew to be mild-mannered people nobody would imagine having been so violent. The widowed bride ended up marrying a third brother from the original family!

The Whitten wedding day massacre of the early 1900s was a legend in Winston County. The passage of almost four decades caused some details to fade into public memory but still left the name Whitten in the public's memory.

Charles told Indy that, as far as he knew, he was not related to these Whittens. Violent drunks with guns were about as far from the family of Willie and Velma as you could get.

That problem being taken care of, my parents' courtship went well. Charles had little money to buy gifts for Indy. They walked together almost every day. As they walked, Charles would find an interesting twig and give it to Indy. He didn't know that she had treasured anything from him and was keeping it in her dorm room.

Indy had two roommates, and they noticed her collections of twigs and teased her about it. Surely, she must be smitten to keep such ordinary things. She was, but this embarrassed her so much that she threw the collection into a trash barrel. After everyone was asleep, she retrieved the twigs and found a good hiding place for them.

Indy brought Charles home to meet her parents around Christmas 1946. The Mitchell farmhouse had a swing on the front porch for "courting and sparking." (My parents never told me about the sparking, whatever that is.). The swing was outside a window that had a curtain. When Charles was talking to Indy, Marie was listening secretly from the other side of the curtain. After Charles left, Marie would imitate the way he walked. She may have thought him to be a city slicker, but at least Indy had marital prospects!

Charles had a part-time job as pastor of a church in Stephensport, Kentucky. When Indy was in Mississippi, and Charles was at his job, he would send her letters. Indy's older brother, Bob, who was 18, would snatch the letters and run out into the fields, often climbing a tree and offering to read the letters to Indy. She followed him, furiously demanding her letters back.

Charles could afford Life Savers, the round candy with a hole in it. When Indy and Charles discussed marriage, he would pretend to place a Lifesaver on her finger as a ring. Of course, nobody's fingers are that skinny! One day, he asked if she wanted a lifesaver and then extended an engagement ring and sunk to one knee to propose. It wasn't a big surprise to Indy, as they had sized her finger before Charles bought the ring. Indy said yes.

The marriage ceremony was on June 1, 1947, at Poplar Flat Baptist Church. Before the ceremony, Charles and Indy had been accepted as missionaries. Charles was offered an appointment in Argentina. Indy was offered an appointment in Argentina or Spain. There must have been some thought they might accept different fields because when they took a group picture of new missionaries, they said Charles and Indy couldn't stand together. Maybe somebody was making a bad joke. When they protested that the marriage was days away, the woman in charge of the pictures said, "There is many a slip between a cup and a lip." My mother found this particularly annoying.

Indy and Charles chose Argentina. A month after the wedding, they were on their way to Colombia for training in the Spanish language.

I Come Into The Picture

My parents studied Spanish intensely in Medellin, Colombia. There were no drug cartels then, but Medellin was a blue-collar town, not a tourist attraction. Before their year of study was completed, there was a political assassination in Bogota. The country was in turmoil, and the mission board was concerned for my parents' safety. They transferred them to Argentina. My older sister Helen was born in 1949 in Mendoza, Argentina, near a mountain that was on the border with Chile.

In 1951 my parents were transferred to work in the seminary in Buenos Aires. A professor was ill, and my dad had a master's in theology. Before my parents went on furlough, there was another illness, the head of the seminary. At 29 years old, my dad was made the temporary head of the seminary.

I was born at the British hospital in Buenos Aires on January 14, 1951. It was a Sunday afternoon, and my parents had to miss the Sunday night service. I never found out if my father was scheduled to preach that night. I had the kind of family where you were teased because your birth caused them to miss church!

I am told that I learned to crawl on a long, enclosed passageway that connected apartments. I have no memory of the 18 months I lived in Buenos Aires before we went on furlough. The four of us left Argentina in 1952 and did not return until 43 years later.

My parents had been gone from their families five years and had two additions to the family, Helen and me. My dad's ambition was to earn a Doctor of Theology at the Louisville seminary. We moved temporarily into student housing in Louisville, on the first floor. I fell out a window and hit my head. It wasn't a long fall. Helen, more than two years old, crawled into my crib and tried to comb my hair with a toy rake. I had a hard skull, so neither incident affected me.

Americans in foreign countries have some skepticism of medical care in their host country. My parents got Helen and me complete physicals in the US. An eye doctor found I was far-sighted and prescribed glasses for me at 18 months old.

This passport picture enabled Helen and Me to return to the US in 1952. It seems obvious from my eyes that I needed glasses.

I am not sure which cartoon character I looked more like Egbert or Mr. Magoo. My father was concerned about my eyesight because at six years old, my father's eyesight was so bad that he was in danger of failing first grade. A visit to the eye doctor and a prescription for glasses, and my father did well in school. As an adult, my father was diagnosed as legally blind in one eye and later as almost completely blind because of wet macular degeneration.

My parents learned that a missionary in Spain was retiring, and the only remaining missionary, J.D. Hughey, was moving to a seminary in Switzerland. Family stories are in conflict here. Either the Mission Board asked my parents to transfer, or my father put out feelers about the job, emphasizing that they were happy in Argentina.

Argentina is a wonderful country and a friendlier place for a Protestant missionary to work than Spain was in 1953. It had been a stressful place for my father. He was made the pastor of a medium-sized church when he hadn't learned Spanish well and had only one sermon in Spanish. His words later were, "It was thrust on me."

My dad was drafted into jobs he wasn't quite ready for, teaching theology in Spanish and later being temporary head of the seminary. I am not saying his skills in speaking Spanish were bad. He became an accomplished preacher in the Spanish language, a problem solver, and a diplomat. In Argentina, he was a junior missionary with many senior missionaries looking over his shoulder. Going to Spain was a welcome change. It turned out to be a gift from God to my parents and to our family.

We Move To Spain

Our trip to Spain was different from our trip to Argentina. In 1953, there weren't long-distance passenger flights. Going to Argentina was a hop, skip, and jump across Central and South America on smaller airplanes. Thankfully I don't have any memory of the return to the US in 1952 since it would have probably included a lot of air sickness.

The only place where an airline could stop going across from New York to Spain would have been the Azores Islands. Our trip to Spain involved an ocean liner. At 30 months old, I have no memory of it either. My parents made friends during a week-long trip across the Atlantic Ocean. The other passengers were tourists or businesspeople. Upon learning that my parents were going to Spain as missionaries, they asked if we knew anybody there. My parents said they didn't. When the boat docked in Barcelona, we were met by Spanish Baptists carrying signs that said "Bienvenido Familia Whitten." (Welcome Whitten Family). J.D. Hughey had returned to Spain temporarily to organize a welcoming party.

My mother was pregnant with my sister Margaret, who was born November 25, 1953. We were the only missionaries in Spain for a couple of months when two more couples arrived. They were Joe and Lila, who had three children, Sylvia, Tony and Janie, and Roy and Joyce Wyatt, who had Michael with them.

Top L to R: Joe Mefford, Lila Mefford, Indy Whitten, me, Charles Whitten and Roy Wyatt. Bottom, L to R Tony Mefford, Janie Mefford, Sylvia Mefford (with her doll), and Helen. Missing: Joyce Wyatt, probably taking care of Michael Wyatt.

My first memory of Spain happened in 1954 when I was three years old. I will continue with what I was told by my parents.

Although there were three missionary couples, only my parents spoke Spanish. My parents were the only teachers in the seminary when it opened up in 1953. As the Meffords and Wyatts learned Spanish, they took over jobs in the Mission. Roy Wyatt became head of the Seminary. Joe Mefford was a talented musician, so he began translation of hymns into Spanish. He also began expanding music in Spanish churches. My father had been handling transfers of money from the Mission Board, so he became mission treasurer. Why? Because nobody else wanted the job. He was saddled with this job for 25 years.

Being a mission treasure involved more than an accountant's duties. In Spain, the treasurer was also the legal representative of an American corporation. In the 1950s and the early 1960s, the Spanish government closed Spanish protestant churches and confiscated their property. Several Spanish pastors were jailed for violating the government's order that their churches be closed.

My dad would pay for new churches and register the properties in the name of the Foreign Mission Board. That protected the properties from confiscation. My father wasn't a lawyer, but he represented the FMB in their contacts with the Spanish government.

My First Memories

Because of my mother's pregnancy in 1953, we hired a nanny. We were referred to a middle-aged woman named Vicenta Ramos. We called her Dona Vicenta, an honorary title. She had an excellent education and had been married to a man with money. When he left her, she was unemployable. We were glad to have her in our home, cooking and taking care of baby Margaret. She loved Margaret and all the kids. If we misbehaved, she never told on us.

One of my first memories was riding a Merry-go-round in Barcelona in 1954. A vendor sold sunflower seeds that we gave to pigeons.

I don't appear to be happy. Maybe a pigeon pecked at me, asking for food. My mother was home taking care of baby Margaret.

I remember getting care packages from the US, with clothes, books, and sometimes American candy. Fragile things were wrapped in American newspapers. I am intrigued by those with colored cartoons on them from the Sunday papers. I couldn't read the papers yet, but I wondered why characters had balloons over their heads. I wondered why my parents would look at them and laugh.

We had a small car which was British, a Morris Minor. My parents sat in the front seats, and the three kids sat behind them. We were small enough that we fit comfortably in the car. The Morris Minor had a small engine. My mother hadn't gotten a driver's license yet. The car was functional when we were in the city, on flat ground. When we tried to drive up a steep incline, the car would slow down and stop. On occasion, my mother had to get out of the car with Helen and me and walk beside the car until the top of the hill! Margaret and my dad would stay in the car.

I never asked my mother why she waited until her 30s to get a driver's license. I remember when she earned it. She took a driver's course and became a driver. She embarked on a long career as an informal chauffeur for dignitaries from the Baptist church who came to Spain. Some said they were scared when my mother was driving. This was teasing. My mother never had an accident in Spain. It was the Madrid traffic they feared.

In 1955, we moved to Madrid. We rented an apartment with a large balcony. Helen, Margaret and I could ride our tricycles there.

Helen, Margaret and Me

Helen turned six in 1955. My mother enrolled her in a Spanish school run by Nuns. Helen spoke fluent Spanish, so this seemed like a good idea at the time. All the instruction was in Spanish, so Helen wasn't taught to read English. Helen came home one day to recite what she had learned in school: "Ave Maria, Purisima…." (Glory to the Virgin Mary, the purest). Baptists admire Mary but do not worship her. My mother didn't want Helen to be confused, so she got her an exemption from catechism classes. At the end of the school year, Helen had learned a lot but couldn't read in English.

Dissatisfied with how Helen's first grade turned out, my mother decided to home-school her. She purchased the curriculum for a correspondence course called the Calvert course. As Helen began second grade, I asked if I could take first-grade classes. I was 5 ½ years old, too young to be admitted into a regular school. My mother remembered her trying to enter school at four years old, and had decided that was not good for herself, so she initially said no to me. I persisted until my parents relented.

Helen and I learned to read English at the same time.

I am showing off my reading skills to Margaret (then 3). Helen is ignoring us

The 1950s were the golden age for vaccines. We had three kids who needed to be stuck with needles, so a local medical clinic sent someone to give us vaccines at home. I got tired of being a human pin cushion. When I learned the Needleman would be coming, I hid under my bed. It wasn't hard to find me. It was a little harder to drag me out from under the bed. I was clutching the legs of the bed as hard as I could. My head bounced off the bottom of the bed on my way out. My arm hurt, and my head hurt too.

My eyes weren't getting any better. My eye doctor diagnosed me with amblyopia. I didn't like the more common name for this condition, lazy eye. My eyes weren't refusing to exercise! They just didn't work together. For years, I was given eye therapy to teach my eyes to cooperate. One eye saw a lion, and the other saw a cage. I was supposed to bring the two together. I thought it was a personal failing that I never brought these images together.

With my persistent eye weakness, I began to identify with a cartoon character named "Mr. Magoo." He was close to blind. He would walk around bumping into things, sometimes doing dangerous things that he escaped through luck. His catchphrase was "Magoo! You've done it again!"

Making Up For Relatives Who Were 3000 Miles Away

Missionaries worked outside the US for 4 or 5 years at a time. Calling loved ones in America was prohibitively expensive and unreliable. Letters took at least a week to cross the ocean. If you had a question, it would take at least 2 weeks to get an answer. We couldn't celebrate Christmas or any other holiday with our US families.

The missionaries decided we kids would call other missionaries "Aunt" and "Uncle." Their kids would be our cousins. This worked out very well. We would visit other missionary families at Christmas time. When we had meetings of all the missionaries, it was a reunion with our cousins, who became our close friends. From the time we went out on the mission field first until the day we returned to the US for college, we spent a lot more time with our missionary cousins than with our biological cousins.

In our first term in Spain, we had acquired four cousins: Sylvia Mefford (born in 1946), Tony Mefford (1948), Janie Mefford (1950), and Mike Wyatt (born 1952). We were closest to the Mefford Kids and our parents were closest to Joe and Lila Mefford.

The Whitten family and the Mefford family had similarities. Each had three kids. We were all expected to be holy rollers, but we weren't.

Later, we would add my brother, John, and the Meffords would add Susie.

Sylvia Mefford was older than Helen by three years. When the Meffords came to Spain, Lila Mefford wrote a study course book for pre-teen Baptist girls called "Sylvia Goes to Spain." My mother wrote study course books but didn't mention any of us in the title. Sylvia went to college in 1964 and was out of our social network.

Tony was one year older than Helen by one year. He was a good-looking, charismatic bad boy, the Fonz, a generation before the Fonz was created in the TV show, Happy Days. He was very popular with girls and admired by everybody. I once accompanied him and one of his friends to a food establishment in Spain that sold alcoholic beverages. ("Bar" didn't have the same negative connotations in Spain that it did in the US). He and his friends bought a chewing gumball from a candy machine. I asked for one. They told me the chewing gum was to hide their tobacco breath! We MKs were not supposed to drink alcohol or smoke. Tony got away with almost anything.

Tony was a lot like his father, Uncle Joe. Uncle Joe and my dad were close friends, but Joe was a treasurer's nightmare. Missionaries were paid for different funds. When they traveled for business, their expenses (supported by receipts) were paid. It was hard to get a receipt out of Uncle Joe. On trips, Joe loved stopping at restaurants. My father tried to save money by our making sandwiches to eat on the trip. Uncle Joe didn't exactly break the rules, but he stretched them. If we kids had the opportunity to travel in the Mefford car, we would jump at the chance. He drove faster than my father and stopped for cokes and food. We loved it.

Janie was more my age. She had straight hair, a little like Joan Baez, who was a famous folk singer at the time. She talked about eating "ruffage," which she had heard from her mother.

She could be acerbic and cynical, but I liked her as a friend. She was a little older than me.

WE RETURN TO THE US IN 1957

We boarded an ocean liner in the summer of 1957 to return to the US. Our arrivals to New York in 1957 and in 1962 tend to blend together in my memories. We enjoyed the ocean cruise. As we approached New York, we were very impressed to pass the Statue of Liberty. New York dazzled us kids. It was a marvelous, multicolored, swirling wonder! Everything seemed to move faster in the US than it had run in Spain.

None of the kids had any memories of the US. Margaret had never been there. Helen was almost four when we left for Spain, and I had been 18 months old. We had very little idea what the United States of America was.

We stayed one night at the Taft Hotel. It was an elegant 1930s-style hotel. We took our meals upstairs and were baffled at the tip required from the people who brought the food. The hotel had air conditioning and a 19-inch TV set, something the kids had never seen before. It showed cartoons, westerns, and other shows. We were very impressed!

Helen, Margaret, and I also experienced something unfamiliar but wonderful - grandparents. My mother's parents, Earl and Marie, lived on a farm. Earl didn't say much and spent most of his time on his crops. Marie cooked and cooked and cooked. She would bring us fudge, and then an hour later, bring us sauerkraut! She also didn't say much. We spent most of our time at their house watching TV.

Willie and Velma were an immediate hit with us. Willie took the three kids to a drugstore in Weir for an ice-cream cone. I had never had ice cream in an edible container. On the way back, I decided to bite the bottom of the cone and suck the ice cream out. I thought it was a good way to eat it. I noticed that Papaw (Willie) was amused at what I was doing. When I finished the cone, he told me not to use that technique again. I was not upset by his mild reprimand. Instead, I was marveling at what an incredible person a grandfather was! Mamaw made incredible peanut butter cookies with imprints on them from a fork. Her voice seemed to have a reassuring purr in it. Mamaw and Papaw were among my favorite people of all time.

While Mamaw and Papaw were catching up with my parents, Margaret and I decided to explore the backyard. Willie had sold his farm and moved into the Presbyterian manse. In his backyard, he built greenhouses. In the spring, he would raise tomato plants and sell them to others in town. This was before large stores would sell starter plants. Papaw had a shed in the back, which was an office for him. He had tools in it. Every important document he had since the 1920s was impaled on a big nail on the wall.

Apparently, Papaw had not used this shed for a while. It had hidden nests of wasps in it. Margaret and I examined Papaw's shed, disturbing the wasps. They attacked both of us at the same time. Margaret and I ran screaming and crying back to the house. We were taken for a bath and for ointments for the stings. Papaw told us not to go into his shed again.

When missionaries returned on furlough, they had to buy a car to get around. During this furlough, my father got in touch with a stateside friend to find him something for us to drive. This friend got a good deal on a Nash. To those who don't know the reputation of the Nash, ignorance is bliss. The car was kind of weird looking, like a bathtub on wheels. It was such a good car that the Nash Corporation stopped making it the year we bought it. The maximum speed to keep it under control was less than 50 MPH. Even at that speed you had loud wind noises. It had poor suspension.

It made you 'Nash' your teeth.

When it broke down, and it broke down a lot, the repair people my dad took it to asked him to park it down the hill because they were embarrassed to have it on their lot. The last straw came when we were doing 40 MPH on a highway. The right front tire broke off its axle and rolled on a hill! It really did. The car tilted toward the right, making loud grinding sounds, and my dad brought it to a halt. My dad vowed to pick his cars on a future furlough and asked us to never hear the word "Nash" again.

We had window air conditioning units in our house to help us deal with the hot Mississippi summer. Helen was in the third grade, and I was in the second grade. My father traveled a lot for presentations on his work in Spain. My uncle, W.A., had earned a degree from the Baptist seminary in New Orleans, so he accompanied my Dad on an extended trip, taking them both out to California for what was called a "school of missions." W.A. was smoking cigarettes on the sly, hoping to keep this from my dad. My dad had a super sense of smell. One day, W.A. came out of the bathroom at a truck stop. My dad said to him,

"I know you are smoking. There is no point in trying so hard to hide it."

IN 1957 westerns were popular on US TV. I became a fan and asked Santa for some Western wear, a holster, and two guns.

Me in my gunslinger phase

There were so many American products that we had not encountered in Spain. My dad bought a bag of marshmallows and burned one over a stove. He offered one to me. With its ash on it, I declined it. My dad insisted, so I brushed aside the ash and tasted the goo. It was good. Marshmallows didn't make it to Spain until I left for college in 1968.

I had surgery on my eyes to try to correct my lazy eye. I stayed overnight at the hospital. I didn't stay overnight at a hospital for more than 60 years.

I enjoyed being in the States so much that I forgot Spanish on that furlough. There were few Spanish speaking people in Mississippi, none that spoke to me. When we returned to Spain, I recovered my Spanish quickly.

Barcelona In 1958

We learned that the Wyatts were transferring to South America. This meant that we would return to Barcelona so that my parents could cover the Seminary until another missionary was ready to replace the Wyatts.

In the year we were on furlough, the Mission Board sent two new Missionary couples. The first was Russell and Patsy Hilliard. They had two small children that I didn't get close to because they lasted less than one term. Their health problems led to them being returned to the US.

The McNeely family had two daughters, Linda, who was six months younger than me, and Marsha, who was a little younger than Margaret. Our first meeting with Linda, then aged 7, did not go well. I do not remember why we clashed. Perhaps she found the three Whitten kids overwhelming. She invited us out on a balcony of her house, reentered her house, and locked us out.

We found this astonishing. The McNeely apartment was on the third floor, so we couldn't climb down to the first floor and re-enter the house by knocking on the front door. We decided to wait. Sure enough, the door was unlocked, and we came back into the McNeely home as if nothing had happened. I reminded Linda of this incident more than 60 years later. She said, "I must have been demented as a child!" I disagreed with her. All the Whitten kids became close friends with Linda and Marsha.

We rented a house outside Barcelona. Helen, Margaret, and I were enrolled in the British school. Our headmaster was named Pickton-Hughes. The school was next to a beach. This made PE more enjoyable. I was in third grade. I became interested in the British flag, known as the "Union Jack." I learned how to draw it.

I remember the British school as quirky but enjoyable. We didn't have a TV set yet. I devoted my spare time to reading books. The school had a contest for who could read the most books. I checked out all the small books I could find in the school library and made sure my teacher gave me credit for reading each. At the end of the year, I had read more books than anybody else in my school. At the graduation, I was given a small book about a fictional pony. It wasn't "My Little Pony" I had earned the book. I treasured that book for almost 50 years until it fell apart due to age.

The school had a Christmas program. Helen. Margaret and I performed a couple of Christmas carols in it. To my chagrin, we were called the "Three Little Kittens" because we were the three little Whittens. I thought this demeaned my masculinity. I went on stage crying, not because of the name but because I had just been given a vaccine, and somebody hit my sore arm.

The Meffords had gone on furlough the year we returned. When they came back to Spain in 1959, we were free to move back to Madrid. We kids had not gotten as attached to Madrid as we would later, but we welcomed the change. In 1958, the US had a naval base in Barcelona. We accepted an invitation from them to tour a submarine and later, an aircraft carrier. The submarine had stairs that went straight up. This represented a hazard to a woman in a dress. Our tour guide said only married sailors were assigned to help women up those stairs. I guess they were more familiar with the view but probably no less interested in it than a single sailor would have been.

We kids had happy memories of Madrid and were glad to make the move. We rented a house in a neighborhood that had many airmen from the US living in the economy. That's what they called airmen who didn't live on the base in Torrejon.

Our house was a three-story brick house. It had a fenced-in elevated yard with a gate wide enough to allow our car to enter the garage and a side gate. We had plenty of space to play. The house was solid brick with no apparent insulation.

Madrid was on a plateau, with what was described as "dry" heat. That didn't keep it from being hot heat in the summer. My bedroom was on the top floor, looking out to the front of the house. At night, the house radiated heat. There were two fans in the house, none of which was assigned to my room. I perspired a lot, trying to fall asleep.

In spite of this, I loved our neighborhood. I found friends who would later be in my classes at the Air Force Dependents Elementary School in central Madrid. Two I remember, Horace Downing and Alan Golacinski. Horace made a name for himself at the end of one school year by running down the street yelling, "I passed! I passed!" Alan Golacinski later entered diplomatic service for the US and was one of the hostages in Teheran in 1979.

Alan, Horace, and I would meet in the neighborhood and have the stereotypically male conversation young male conversation: "What do you want to do?" "I don't know. What do you want to do?" "I don't know…." We were not an imaginative group.

We could ride our bikes around the neighborhood. Both of my parents were gone from the house in our first couple of years. I became bolder in riding my bike. I took a wrong turn one time and went further and further from home. Finally, I realized that I was all the way downtown at a statue of a bear trying to get fruit out of a tree. The Spanish people called it "El oso robando las uvas" (The bear stealing grapes). I turned around and slowly retraced my steps, arriving home two hours after our usual suppertime. I told my mother about my mistake, and she didn't punish me.

My mother didn't know that in my explorations, I had found a hole leading to a small cave. The other boys with me were unwilling to go into the cave. I crawled into it and noticed how confining it was. It dawned on me that if it collapsed on me, I might disappear from everyone's lives. I slowly crawled backward out of it. The Good Lord protected this reckless little boy.

Mamaw And Papaw Make A Visit

In 1959, we had been gone from Mississippi for 10 of the last 12 years. Papaw had gone on Social Security in 1958. His truck farming business had prospered enough that he could afford a trip to Spain to see what the mission field was like.

Mamaw and Papaw took an ocean cruise from New York to south Spain in the summer of 1959. I imagine he found New York city as foreign as he later found the cities of Europe. We were delighted to have them visit us.

In the US, I had little influence or power when I was with Papaw. In Spain, I knew Spanish and he didn't. I was delighted to accompany him on walks, and to translate for him. Papaw decided he wanted to plant tomatoes in our yard. He asked me to help him find fertilizer for the plants. I took him through fields until we found a sheep herder with his flock of sheep. The sheep had done their business. Papaw gave me 25 pesetas (which was about 50 cents) and told me to offer it to the sheep herder for the sheep poop. The sheepherder looked puzzled and then laughed. "Por la basura?" (for the trash?) We didn't have to pay.

I accompanied Papaw for any whim he had. I would go with him to a grocery store where he would pick up a chicken. Papaw had developed a taste for a Spanish dish, which actually came from North Africa, called Paella. It is a rice dish with rice colored yellow. It has vegetables in it with any combination you like of beef, lamb, pork or seafood. To get the rice crunchy, you could bury it below ground with a fire over it, like a Hawaiian Luau. We cooked it on a stove.

Papaw would give me money to buy a couple chickens, and then would take it home to set down in front of our nanny with the word "paella!" This is one of two Spanish words he mastered, the other being "GRACIAS," which is thank you. The way he said it, it sounded like he was growling.

We Take Willie And Velma On A Tour Of Europe

Every few years, Baptist missionaries in Europe would meet in Switzerland for a general conference. The two countries in Europe with the most missionaries were Spain and Italy. There were at least two missionaries in Portugal, France, Germany, and Switzerland.

Switzerland was the site for a very nice Seminary at Ruschlikon, which was located on the banks of Lake Zurich. It was a super mission meeting for the MKs. We took Mamaw and Papaw with us to the conference, with the plan to visit other countries.

Papaw was interested in observing farming in European countries. We stopped for him to see what kind of cows they had. We bought fresh bread, tomatoes, and bologna sandwiches.

Switzerland is a beautiful country, with mountains and valleys to admire. At the seminary, Mamaw and Papaw watched us while my parents participated in conferences.

We traveled from Switzerland to Rome, Italy. There are many interesting places to visit in Italy, but Rome is the interesting to a Christian. On the way, my father sang "Arrivederci Roma" and pretended to be speaking in French and German, languages he didn't speak. 1959 was still the era of Elvis. My Dad preferred Perry Como.

We saw the Coliseum in Rome. We visited a prison where the apostle Paul was supposed to have been kept. As we descended some concrete stairs, our guide showed us a dent in the wall caused by Paul's tripping and hitting his head. This stretched credibility even for the 8-year-old I was. We saw the catacombs where Christians hid during a period of persecution.

Of course, we toured the Vatican. It is an incredible site, next to the Sistine Chapel, filled with statues and paintings. While there I got separated from my family. After searching for them, I realized that my Italian was not good enough to ask that they be paged. Luckily, I remembered where we had parked. I returned to the car and waited for the others. They were happy to see me there.

After considerable travel, it was time for us to return to Spain. Mamaw and Papaw had a date to return on the ocean liner in South Spain.

None of us realized that we were facing a tragedy that could have upended our family.

The Auto Accident Of September 4, 1959

We arrived in Barcelona on September 3, 1959. The seminary had beds for us to sleep in. The next day would be my dad's 37th birthday. We would drive 10 hours to Madrid and then make the final plans to take Mamaw and Papaw to their ship in South Spain.

We had driven from Barcelona to Madrid many times. It was 600 kilometers, around 360 miles. Our Seat didn't get great mileage, particularly with seven people in it. We would be lucky to average 40 miles per hour.

The drive on September 4 was a dreary one. It was raining most of the day. At noon, we had hoped to stop to make sandwiches, but there were no dry places to stop. My mother had fallen asleep with Margaret leaning on her. In the back row, Papaw was at the left window, with me next to him, and Helen on the left of Mamaw, who was at the other window seat.

We were on a two-lane road, with many trucks ahead of us and behind us. We had seen minor accidents along the way. A Mack truck going the opposite direction as is decided to pass another truck. The first thing my father did was the truck coming directly at us. My dad jerked the car to the right, and the truck sped up to make it back into his lane. He didn't make it. He hit our car at full speed on the left corner of our car, smashing our front and hurling my dad toward his steering wheel. This was before the time of mandatory seat belts. They were not installed on Spanish-built cars. My dad was gravely injured.

Papaw opened his door. He and I were the first out of the car. The front end was smoking. It was bashed in. I could hear my dad groaning from inside the car. My legs were shaking as I tried to assess the damage to our car.

Helen, Margaret, and I had no injury, nor did Papaw. My mother's head had been slumped down as she slept. Her face hit the dash on the right side. The drawer of the glove compartment had sliced through one of her eyelids but hadn't damaged her eye. Her eyelid bled copiously. She kept asking what had happened.

Mamaw saw the truck bearing down on us and had braced one arm and one leg to keep herself from flying forward. Both limbs had a broken bone.

Our accident happened perhaps 30 miles from a town called Zaragoza. The Korean War had resulted in dramatic improvements to emergency care, but those improvements hadn't been instituted in Spain. Papaw and I stood outside the car, wondering what would happen next. It was around 1:30 P.M. Our car was still on the road. Cars were slowly edging by us but not stopping. My father was in bad pain, bleeding internally. My mother and Mamaw stayed in the car.

About 30 minutes after the accident, two cars stopped to help us. One was a large car with a folding middle seat. I always loved riding in taxis that had this arrangement. The other was a smaller car. Neither was an emergency vehicle. Men from the larger car pulled the driver's side open to our car and helped my dad walk to their vehicle. That must have been a nightmare of pain for him. The other six of us crowded into both cars. They took us to the closest medical facility, which was a clinic.

The clinic didn't have a doctor or nurse there. My dad was placed on a gurney, where he continued to groan. The clinic didn't have any medication stronger than an aspirin. Margaret said she was tired. The clinic workers, who apparently lived in the back of the facility, boiled some potatoes and fed them to us kids.

It was obvious dad was bleeding internally. The clinic made some calls to hospitals to pick him up. The US had a recently opened Air Force base in Zaragoza. Since my dad was American, they thought this would be the best for him.

Time passed quickly as the clinic tried to make arrangements for the Armed Forces hospital to come pick us up. Knowing that there were seven of us, they made arrangements for two ambulances to pick us up. The most modern of the ambulances got lost and never made it to our clinic. The older one took quite a while to find our clinic, arriving just before 5 P.M. My father had been bleeding from his internal injuries. The most serious was a crushed appendix, which could have resulted in his bleeding out.

We managed to cram the seven of us into that ambulance. My mother sat in the back by my father, and I sat beside her. My dad was going in and out of consciousness. At one point, I asked my mother, "Will Daddy live?" My mother said, "I don't know. We must pray for him." I told her that I had already begun praying for him.

My mother later wrote a small book titled "We Camped at Heaven's Gate" to describe our experiences. A lot of my memories come from her book. On the cover, it showed a tent outside a city with a gate.

We arrived at the base a little before 6 P.M. My father was in the emergency room and prepared for immediate surgery. The doctors discovered that my father had extensive blood loss and needed a lot of blood to replace his losses. They also learned that his blood type was

A negative, a rare blood type. There was little of this blood in their blood bank.

This was one of several near miracles that led to my dad's survival from the accident. The base opened its FM radio station for the first time 15 minutes after my dad entered the hospital. The first announcement on the radio was for donations of A-positive blood. Enough airmen lined up that my dad got the blood he needed to survive the hours long surgery.

The armed forces had made great strides in trauma medicine, helping our wounded in the Korean War. The surgeon who operated on my dad wasn't trained in Korea. He had enough training to do the complicated surgery my dad needed. When my dad was recovering, the doctor told him that he did some of the surgery while reading from a textbook!

My dad's spleen was removed, and bleeding from it stopped. My dad had many systems damaged by the accident. Contents of his stomach had been splashed all over his insides. Leaving any particle would have led to potentially fatal infections. They very carefully picked out all the particles and closed the bleeding in my dad's chest. Early in the morning of the 5th of September, the surgeon closed my dad up and sent him to recovery. He told my mother that he had all he could and the rest was up to God. He opened my dad's chest from his breastbone to his navel. The recovery left my dad with a "zipper" that embarrassed him a little when he wore a bathing suit.

While the surgery began, the rest of the family were seated in chairs near the emergency room, the kids near my mother. Here is the second near miracle. We were all in shock, my mother with her clothes covered with blood and my grandparents worrying about my Dad and grandma. My mother went to a treatment room and got stitches in her eyelid. My grandmother began the process of fixing her broken bones.

What would we do? We had no clothes other than what was on us. We had no place to stay. My mother wasn't leaving the hospital until she got news of my dad.

The Baptist denomination published a small devotional magazine titled "The Open Window." After a three-paragraph devotional, it listed missionaries who had birthdays on the day of the devotional. My father's crisis happened on the day his birthdate was listed, when many Baptists would be praying for him, not knowing his need. One of those who prayed for him was an airman's wife at the Zaragoza base.

This woman, whose name was Graham, was originally from Mississippi. She kept track of missionaries who came from Mississippi and knew generally that one of those was in the country where her husband had been assigned. On the day of the accident, she had read my father's name.

Mrs. Graham had attended a church in Mississippi where my mother spoke, so she had a memory of what she looked like. On the day of the accident, she had forgotten to pick up medicine for one of her kids and came by the hospital late. As she passed the seats where we were sitting, she did a double take. It looked like Indy Whitten was sitting in her hospital. She approached us hesitantly, seeing that we were in distress, and asked, "Are you a missionary?" My mother said, "Yes."

After learning about the accident, Mrs. Graham asked where we would be staying. When she learned that we had no place to stay, she insisted that we stay at her home. It was an incredibly generous offer. She was a God send. She packed the three kids and my grandparents into her car and took us home. After giving us food, she put us to bed.

When my dad came out of anesthesia, he asked a nurse if they had a choir rehearsing near the hospital. When they said no, my dad said he had heard the most beautiful hymns being sung. This was apparently a point where he was about to ascend to heaven if the surgeon had not brought him back. A third miracle came in the fact that so many people were praying for my dad in his time of need. We always read the Open Window at breakfast. My parents would consider the point of the devotional. Then, they would read the names of the missionaries having birthdays before they prayed. Unlike a lot of people who read the names of strangers and then prayed for them as a group, my parents would stop to mention the people they knew and where they had met them! God knew my father's needs even if a lot of people didn't. Prayers are not answered because of the number of people praying the same prayer, but it is not insignificant.

The Associated Press ran a story about a Missionary in Spain who had a devastating accident and was being treated at an Armed forces hospital in Spain. My Uncle W.A. got the news and immediately called Gov. J.P. Coleman, who knew our family. Coleman called the two Mississippi Senators, Eastland and Stennis, and asked them to get information from the Department of Defense. Congressional interest always makes government employees work a little harder to do their jobs right.

We stayed at Mrs. Graham's house for two weeks. She was a good cook and a strict mother. She led me to the bathroom and told me to take a bath. I was a little uncertain about getting naked in a stranger's house, so I ran into the water but didn't get in. When I left the bathroom, I had forgotten to let the water out. Mrs. Graham insisted that I actually come into water and soap. We were told that my dad's surgery had been successful and that he was recovering slowly. The armed forces hospital adhered to a rule of 12 years old minimum for visitors. I was not allowed to see my dad then or on his recovery at a Madrid hospital later. I was very attached to my dad and didn't want to lose him.

We Go American In 1960

My grandparents accompanied Helen, Margaret and me back to Madrid. We enrolled in the armed forces dependent's school that was located off a busy street leading to downtown Madrid. I was in the fourth grade, Helen was in the fifth, and Margaret was in the first grade. We had felt ourselves to be British in Barcelona. In Madrid, going to an American school, we reveled in being American.

My dad spent a month in the Zaragoza base hospital and another month in the British American hospital in Madrid. I accompanied my mother when she visited him. I was not allowed to go to my dad's room there, so I camped out in the hospital library and read almost all their books. I developed an affinity for Penguin Books, which was a British paperback publishing company.

I read all I could about American politics. I began with Teddy Roosevelt, a charismatic American president, and continued to other Presidents. My dad was a Republican. In his youth he had appreciated FDR and what the New Deal did for Mississippi when he was growing up. World War II made Dwight Eisenhower his hero.

I was not happy that six weeks after the accident, I wasn't allowed to see my dad. My dad realized this and worked hard to build up the energy to walk down a hall. When the day came, I ran down the hallway and embraced him gently. He was wearing a green housecoat that was obviously bought at the hospital store. He looked so fragile. I loved him so much and was glad that I wouldn't be separated from him for much longer.

Our nanny (I hate calling her "maid"), Dona Vicenta, came to take care of us as soon as the kids returned to Madrid. She stayed with us until we were able to hire another nanny. My parents learned of a 30-year-old woman from Galicia (the northeast part of Spain, named Rita Duran.

R to L Margaret, Rita, John and Helen

She became so close to us that it was like having a relative in the house. That had a good and bad part to it. The bad was that when my mother wanted to entertain people at the house, she had to get Rita's permission! Rita attended an Assemblies of God church. Her religious fervor made us look like liberals in comparison!

After my dad came home, he was under instructions from his doctor to take it easy. He still had a lot of internal injuries that needed to heal. The strain of not being able to do his job and being a part-time dad at best led him to a duodenal ulcer. In 1960, this was a much bigger deal than it is today. He was put on further bedrest with a bland diet.

Today, we don't connect ulcers with stress or spicy foods. It is caused by a "bacteria" called H-Pylori, which can be treated with antibiotics. In my adulthood, I have been diagnosed with ulcers three times, and each treatment seems to take it less seriously than the other. The last time, my doctor gave me a 10-day supply of antibiotics and scheduled a follow-up appointment. I didn't need it.

In early 1960, we discovered that my mother was pregnant again (and for the last time). Both of my parents were 38 years old, relatively old for a baby. I did not give any thought to the reasons for their conception seven years after Margaret's birth. It struck me later that when they saw my dad would recover from the operation, this seemed like a good time.

We got a subscription to the Stars and Stripes, the newspaper for all the military overseas. The Spanish newspapers were controlled by the dictator, Franco. We were pleased to read a relatively uncensored paper. (It wasn't allowed to criticize the military). It had American comics like Peanuts and Lil' Abner. It also had sports scores.

In 1960, I developed an interest in baseball that has never gone away. One of our regular visitors was a Swedish Baptist named Erik Ruden. When he visited us in early 1960, I told him stories about American politics. He vowed to read up on this so that he could converse with me. A year later, when he offered to discuss politics with me, I told him that I now wanted to discuss baseball.

From knowing little about baseball when we were in the US last, I became an aficionado. The most exciting team was the Yankees. They had been in the World Series every year that I was alive except for 1954 and 1959. Their most exciting player was Mickey Mantle. I read everything I could about the Yankees and Mantle.

I didn't just read. For Christmas 1960, I asked Santa for a baseball glove and a baseball. Santa generously threw in a bat too. My dad accompanied me out to a soccer field not far from our house and pitched to me. After missing a few times, I made contact and felt that I had talent!

In 1961, I signed up for a team of 10–12-year-olds called the Toros. (The Bulls). I got a shirt and a hat. I spent hours bending a V in the hat's bill, which I thought was necessary. I had spent much of my free time pounding the ball into my glove to create the sweet spot where I would catch the ball.

The Toros were a great experience for me. My eye problems made it difficult for me to figure out where a fly ball would land. I also was not a great hitter. I was a great teammate. The coach placed me in the outfield. He understood that in the rare event, a ball was hit to me, I would probably pick it up after it stopped rolling and fling it in the direction of the infield. By that point, the runner would be rounding third base. Difficulties handling the ball created what is derisively called a "little league home run."

We had good pitching, good enough to carry us to the championship game of our division. It seemed to me like the 7th game of the World Series. We built up a lead of 12-9 in the last inning. Our best pitcher had to be taken out because of pitch limitations created to protect kids' arms. The replacement pitcher gave up four runs, and we lost.

Team moms had brought a chocolate cake for the celebration. It was good, but we were still sad. We sat on the bench eating chocolate cake and crying. We wouldn't get a championship trophy. If you didn't win the final game, you got no trophy.

My father returned to his job as Mission treasurer, and as a church planter in the Madrid area. We had Spanish friends as well as those I went to school with at the military dependent's schools.

I enjoyed being invited by Spanish families to accompany them to a fiesta. Usually, they had a son my age. My stays in Spanish homes bring back olfactory memories. Most Spanish apartment houses have an enveloping smell of olive oil, which is used in cooking and in salads. At a fiesta, I was mesmerized by the carny games, by almond candies and by the friendship these families offered me.

We were a few blocks from Plaza Peru, a roundabout that led to downtown. Plaza Peru had fresh foods that we would buy. Giant grocery stores didn't come to Spain until I left for college. Diagonally across the street was a long street with a 10-foot concrete fence that provided privacy to what went on at "Sevilla Films." Many multi-million-dollar movies were made there. Dr Zhivago was one of them. I only saw the inside of Sevilla Films once. It was in my senior year when they made "Guns for the Magnificent Seven." The original Magnificent Seven movie had been magnificent, but its remakes were not. They asked for extras. I went and offered my services. I was deemed too short in height and in the length of my hair. My friend, Mark Singer, was chosen. In one scene, he was to antagonize the actor George Kennedy. Kennedy was supposed to knee him in the crotch. This scene was repeated several times. I hope that Singer was wearing a sturdy athletic supporter.

I was most interested in an English-language movie theatre run by the military. I didn't have a military dependent's ID card, so I had to take a friend with me who had one. When I didn't have one, I would ask a random stranger to buy my ticket. I usually got in.

Spanish movie theaters were very good. There were many of them usually playing American or British films dubbed into Spanish. The tickets were inexpensive. They used lemon spray to cover body odors common to crowds. I still associate lemon spray with the good times I had at Spanish movies. The best place for movies was on Jose Antonio Street, in downtown Madrid. With its movie marquees up and down the street, it looked a little like Broadway in New York.

The best of the theaters were the new Cinerama theaters. They had a huge screen that was extended out on the left and right, creating a 180-degree screen. The first we ever attended was the showing of "How the West Was Won." We arrived late and had to sit in the front row. I got a stiff neck looking up at the incredible action. When they showed a raft about to go over a waterfall, I felt I was about to be swept away in the water. When George Peppard was hanging off a loose log on a runaway train, I experienced vertigo.

Movies were a regular family event for us. My parents didn't want to pay more for treats than they had for entrance. My mother would bring a large shopping bag with sandwiches and drinks. When the theater got dark, my mother would assemble the sandwiches and hand them out. Although we were violating theater rules, this part was safe.

The risky part was the drinks. My mother had plastic cups, a Coke and a drink called "Gaseosa" in Spain. It was carbonated water with a pressure greater than a Sprite. Sometimes, the pressure was so great that the glass in the bottle would shatter. Because of the potential injury, gaseosa bottles were often carried in a plastic sleeve.

Gaseosa and Coke mixed well. When my mother opened the gaseosa bottle, it made a distinctive sound. My mother had waited until the usher was on the other side of the room. The usher would return and focus his flashlight on our aisle. We never got caught.

While we were in Madrid, my dad had to sign for some papers in the Canary Islands, which was off North Africa. The Canary Island was not known for its Canaries, but for its dogs. In Latin, Canus means dog. He decided to make this a family vacation.

We would have enjoyed the trip more if Margaret hadn't caught chicken pox from friends. Helen, Margaret and I came down with it as we were settling in a hotel. My mother had to entertain us there for a week. She got a box, two large cardboard rolls and a long roll of butcher paper. With it she pasted pictures on the roll to make a story. We had a do-it-yourself TV. I was very impressed at my mother's ingenuity.

John was born on December 24, 1960. Before his birth we had met as a family to decide what name he would have. John was a consensus first name. I wanted to call him "John Henry." Henry was a family name, but John Henry seemed too colloquial. We put names in a hat and ended up with John William Whitten. My middle name was my father's first name. John's was Dad's middle name.

We were so excited to announce John's birth that we made a phone call to Mamaw and Papaw. We told the operator what time we wanted to place the call. Our afternoon would be morning their time. We kid had one line each. We had one phone in my parent's bedroom and one in the living room downstairs. We set up a tape recorder to memorialize the call. On the recording, you hear us, and then you hear us stomping down the stairs to turn off the tape recorder.

I was glad we had a boy. This evened out our family at two boys and two girls. That was the way God intended it.

Dad Helps Create An English Language Church Of Military Personnel

In 1961, airmen from the Torrejon Air Force Base approached my father and asked for help in forming a Baptist church that would be outside the base. This would be a new question for my dad. He said that before they proceed, they would need permission from the base hierarchy. If they vetoed it, it would be impossible to proceed.

Why would members of the military want a church when the military provided a variety of chaplains for everyone's religious needs? There were ministers for Protestants, priests for Catholics and Rabbis for Jewish military personnel. Each religious group had differences between members. Catholics would attend a general mass. Jews would similarly attend a service with a Rabbi. Baptists weren't comfortable in a generic protestant service.

There were so many Protestant groups, Baptists, Methodists, Presbyterians, etc, that it was impractical for the military to give each group their own church.

The airmen approached the base commander. He said he didn't have any objection to their project but that he would have to look at it when the final details were determined. My father was pleasantly surprised when he approached the Spanish civil authorities that they didn't care where or how Americans worshipped. They got around about a church being formed off-base for military personnel, and a chaplain objected. Perhaps he was worried that his Sunday attendance would drop, and the base would decide his services were not needed anymore. When the Base commander learned that Spanish authorities had no objection, he overruled any objections by the chaplain and approved the project.

The next step in developing the new church was to find a pastor. The organizers petitioned the Foreign Mission Board to appoint a missionary for their church. The FMB told them that developing a missionary for this duty would take at least two years. They suggested my father would be a good candidate. The church organizers were pleased since he was their first candidate. My dad accepted the job.

Pastoring an English-language church didn't replace the duties my dad already had. He still had to balance the books and travel around Spain, signing for church properties. My dad had barely recovered from the auto accident and from a bout of ulcers. Still, he agreed to add the new duties. A church committee found a building that seemed more than adequate. It was a three-story duplex located on the North side of Madrid. A survey had predicted an anticipated 200 members for the new church. The walls separating the two apartments were knocked out so that people could move freely. On the top floor, they created a long room with a side room that faced the pulpit. This created an auditorium that fit 250 folding chairs.

The basement garage had a grease pit used to change oil. Bricklayers were brought in to build up walls around it so that it would accommodate water. This created a baptistry. The workers were confused about what they were doing and referred to this as a "Piscina pequena" (a small swimming pool).

The church was named "Immanuel," which meant "God with us." At 10 years old, I thought it should be Emmanuel. I learned that in Hebrew, God's name starts with an 'I'. The church opened with enthusiasm and quickly grew to more than 150 members. The church voted to join the Spanish Baptist Association (the UEBE) and to contribute part of their tithes to Spanish missions, and the Lottie Moon Christmas offering for missions around the world.

We three kids were enthusiastic about the church. It wasn't that we didn't like attending Spanish Baptist churches. Our problem was that we never stayed in one church long enough for our own spiritual growth. My parents had taught in the Seminary off and on for almost ten years. Some of the pastors had been their students. Preaching in front of my father had a little intimidation for them, like teaching a class in college with your major professor watching.

We lived in two cities, Barcelona and Madrid, which had multiple Baptist churches. If we stayed in one church, it might look like we preferred that church over the others in town. My parents solved these problems by creating new churches. We would stay there for months, and when this mission point was ready, to call a Pastor and move on to a new project.

Immanuel offered Helen, Margaret and me the chance to grow spiritually. Baptist churches usually give an altar call at the end of the sermon. This is an invitation to acknowledge that you are a sinner and to accept Jesus as your savior. Helen had already made her profession of faith. My parents were wary of us making this commitment before we understood what we were doing. On one of the first services, Margaret and I came forward to make our professions of faith. We were among the first to be baptized in the converted grease pit.

Immanuel offered Sunday school classes for our age groups and groups for boys and girls, the Royal Ambassadors for boys and the Girl's Auxiliary for girls. We became involved in all activities of the church, sometimes coming 7 days a week.

I particularly enjoyed the music programs of Immanuel. In Spanish churches, the music was provided by a small organ pumped by your feet. We were given a small hymn book with the lyrics but no music in it. There are several well-known hymns that I remember best for its Spanish lyrics, not English. Singing tended to drag in tempo, particularly when the audience was mostly old people.

We used the Broadman hymnal, with music accompanying the lyrics. Having the music meant that any pianist could play along with the singing. As I developed my skills as a pianist, I began accompanying the singing service at church. I was proud to accompany my dad to the Saturday morning men's workday. They served a variety of pork products, bacon, sausage, and ham, like my grandparents' breakfast. I didn't give too much attention until 35 years later when I married a woman who was a member of the Seventh Day Adventist church. They don't eat pork.

The Spanish civil authorities underestimate the potential of an English language church in the population of Madrid. In addition to the military population at the base, there was a large expatriate population in Madrid who were also looking for a church. Spanish people who spoke English (or wanted to) came to the church. The word of Immanuel's existence spread around Madrid, particularly after Immanuel built a large sign advertising its services. Spanish-speaking churches in Spain were forbidden to have signs outside identifying their existence. It would be almost 20 years before they got that right.

During Immanuel's history, the first flowers of religious freedom began to blossom in Spain. By the 1980s, after the death of Franco, Spanish protestant churches were allowed to advertise their presence publicly. The base at Torrejon was closed, but Immanuel continued to worship in English.

We Learn About Racism On Our 1962 Furlough

We completed a four-year term in 1962. In the summer of 1962, we traveled to a town in Italy, Santa Severa, for a missionary conference. Sometimes, I marvel at how much trust the missionaries gave to their kids of all ages, left to their own devices while the parents were meeting in a hotel conference room.

The hotel where we were staying was next to a beach. It was not a very good beach, thin with gritty sand. It also had a stream emptying into the sea. We older MKs (I was 11) took the younger kids with us and began making sandcastles and other sculptures you make on the beach. We had a lot of fun!

On a lunch break, some parents went looking for their kids. They found, to their profound shock, that the stream emptying into the sea was raw sewage! It didn't smell good, but those of us who lived on seacoasts found the smell familiar. My excuse was that I had inherited a poor sense of smell from my mother! The parents found somebody else to watch their younger kids besides the older MKs.

We were returning to us for the first time since 1958 and the first time since our accident. We gave up our house in Madrid and took an ocean liner from Barcelona to New York. Helen was 13, and Margaret was closing in on 9 years old. John, at age 1, would be seeing the US for the first time. We had been assured by letters that Mamaw had healed from injuries in the accident, but we wanted to see that for ourselves.

We were greeted at the airport in Jackson, Mississippi, by many of our relatives on both sides of the family. Papaw and Mamaw were there, as were my mother's brothers, Bruce and H.C. and their spouses and children. Everybody was four years older and a varying number of pounds heavier. We drove up an artificial lake which had been created in our absence, the Ross Barnett reservoir. It was named after one of the most virulent racists in Mississippi politics, probably because he was the governor. Our caravan stopped for cold watermelon. We didn't have that in Spain.

Our one-year home was in Clinton again, several blocks down the street from where we had rented a house in 1957. A developer named Byrd had built a number of houses, taking one for himself and moving his house and setting it up on blocks on a lot just off a busy highway.

I had become a big baseball fan. I used my allowance each week to buy baseball cards. I was frustrated that in a year of collecting, I did not get one for Mickey Mantle or Henry Aaron. At the end of the year, I took a large collection back to Spain.

I wasn't able to get on a baseball team, but I tried to keep my baseball skills (such as they were) sharp. College Avenue ended at my house. There was a big sign in front of our house telling people to turn right or left. I would spend hours throwing rocks at the sign, trying to improve my accuracy.

One day, while my parents were taking a nap and the three older kids were watching TV, John decided to take a walk outside. He was two years old. When we realized he was no longer in the house. We were scared he would walk out on Highway 80 and get hit by a car. We woke our parents up, and we all ran frantically in all directions, yelling his name.

After a half hour of our anxiety, John's face appeared on a ventilation screen underneath the house. We were very relieved. My parents went back to bed without trying to figure out which one of us had failed to keep a watch on John.

We older kids actually liked taking care of John. When the church was over, the three of us would run down to the nursery to get John. At home, we would take control of him to the exclusion of the others. Once Margaret took John into the bathroom and locked the door. The lock was a latch. I took a kitchen knife and flipped the latch. Once the door was open, I saw Margaret sitting on the toilet. I grabbed John and took him with me. I will never forget the look on her face!

With each furlough, my parents seemed to be assigned more speaking engagements. In the Spring of 1963, they received a request to speak at a small church in the town of "It," Mississippi. As you approached the town you saw a sign that said "This is It." A couple of blocks later, the sign said, "That was It."

My parents hated to turn down any requests. This request was harder for them because the preacher of that church was Mamaw's older brother, Richard Eddleman, whom we called "Uncle Dick." He was old, and his vision and hearing were impaired. When I visited Uncle Dick, and his third wife, Edna, he would sometimes confuse me with the paper boy. My parents had a conflict on the date, so they sent me to speak.

At 12 years old I had heard my parents' speech many times. My parents gave me a set of their slides and a slide projector and sent me to speak. I did a decent job presenting Missions in Spain, using punch lines that my parents used and eliciting amens and laughs as appropriate. Uncle Dick lavished me with praise. He said my dad was a better preacher than his son, Leo Eddleman. Leo had been a missionary in Israel and had also been President of the Baptist seminary in New Orleans. When I told this to my dad, he laughed and said that Uncle Dick was a great flatterer.

Racism In 1962

Two major events happened in 1962 that affected our TV watching. There was the Cuban Missile Crisis. Our country was on the brink of nuclear war with Russia. That preempted the Beverly Hillbillies and other westerns. I was in 7th grade, but I didn't know enough to be scared.

I was more involved with the second event, the integration of the University of Mississippi, by a black man named James Meredith. I was baffled initially by Mississippi resisting his admissions. Eight years earlier, the Supreme Court had integrated public schools. Why not allow Meredith in to Ole Miss?

We had some contact with black kids in Spain. A large percentage of servicemen were black. Each of us had some black friends. We had all gone to school with them. We had only run into racism in 1959 when somebody used the "N" word to make fun of black classmates. Skin color meant little to us. Spain was invaded by North African Muslims and was partially occupied from the 11th century to the 15 century. Spanish people intermarried with the invaders, leaving Spanish to be described as "olive skin." Variations in skin color didn't bother us.

James Meredith was denied admission to Ole Miss because he was black. He sued in federal court, and the court ordered Ole Miss to admit him. The whole Mississippi government resisted the court order. Governor Barnett called up the National Guard to prevent civil unrest. President Kennedy sent in federal marshals to protect James Meredith.

The conflict between Federal and State officials was mostly theater. Behind the scenes, the National Guard agreed to stand down.

Barnett insisted on being forced to step aside. He wanted to have a gun pointed at him by a federal marshal. This was denied because it was too inflammatory.

Our family friend, J.P Coleman, had been Barnett's predecessor in the Governor's office. I don't know how he would have handled this incident, but I believe he would not have showboated and incited people to violence. The standdown was bad for Mississippi's reputation.

I was disgusted at Barnett's behavior. He seemed to be inciting violent behavior. Years later, three civil rights workers were kidnapped and murdered by people who were incited by Barnett.

My social studies teacher at Clinton Middle School asked us what we thought of the going on in Oxford, Mississippi. I was shocked that there was a unanimous condemnation of JFK for sending in troops and forcing white students to go to school with one black man. The rights of white people were being trampled on! A black college student would lower standards at Ole Miss and be a threat to white women there. The Kennedys were Yankees and no better than the carpetbaggers who flocked to the South after the Civil War. If anybody in class disagreed, they kept their opinions to themselves, probably out of self-preservation.

Kids my age in 1962 Mississippi didn't go against the crowd, not when they could be ostracized or beat up. None but me, naive me. I raised my hand and said JFK had no other choice. As President, he was required to enforce laws and support federal rulings. What was wrong, I asked, with going to school with a black person? I had done this in Spain.

The result was a torrent of angry responses and hate. As a stranger in Mississippi (a Yankee?) I wasn't aware of how what black people were really like. Black people, they informed me, were disgusting, dirty and dumb. They only cared for one thing. At 11, I didn't know what that one thing was. Education? Good jobs? Friends? They all agreed that black people should stay in their place.

In a few minutes, I had gone from being the son of an admired missionaries to a pariah. Girls waking by me hissed, "nigger lover." I asked, "Doesn't the Bible say we should love our neighbor?" Their answer was that black people were not their neighbors.

I wasn't beat up. I was ignored. I was shy at this age and didn't expect to make lifelong friends in Clinton, so I didn't miss having friends in the 7th grade. Every day, I would watch afternoon programs after school: Wyatt Earp, Gunsmoke and the Texan. At night we enjoyed the Beverly Hillbillies and the Flintstones. The Beverly Hillbillies were a huge hit. Even though the characters played dumb, this was one of the first shows introducing the mainstream to Southern culture. The Flintstones was the first cartoon show to be broadcast in prime time.

Prior to our return to Spain, both of my parents took a trip for speaking engagements and left the kids in the care of Papaw and Mamaw. An important letter arrived from the Foreign Mission Board. My father called and asked Papaw to open the letter and read it on the phone. The letter informed us that we were assigned to Barcelona in 1963 to replace missionaries on furlough. When we heard this, Helen, Margaret and I burst into tears. We loved Madrid and didn't want to live in Barcelona. The Navy base there had closed. Barcelona water tasted bad (it had a metallic taste). They spoke a language we didn't understand (Catalan). We wanted to go back to our friends and the traditions we had in Madrid. My grandparents were very concerned. They called my father back to ask if this decision could be changed. My dad said he doubted. My parents always wanted to serve where they were needed. We had to dry our tears and prepare to live in Barcelona.

When we got on the ocean liner in New York, I felt a sense of relief. I didn't have to live in Mississippi. I vowed to myself to never return if I had a choice. We had a great time on the ship as a family. I remember watching a movie with Anthony Quinn and Mickey Rooney titled "Requiem for a Heavyweight." It was a boxing movie about an aging boxer who loses to an upstart young pugilist. The young boxer was played by an unknown named Cassius Clay who was later to change his name to Muhammed Ali. I had no idea at the time the influence Ali would have on my life.

I Begin To Grow Up

Barcelona proved to be more fun than we had expected it to be. We were enrolled at the American School of Barcelona. So was Linda McNeely. She became fast friends with all of us. For the first time, we had a music teacher. She told us that rock and roll was fun and games but wouldn't last. I had not given much attention to popular music at the time. I didn't know much about Buddy Holly or Elvis, but I liked the Everly Brothers. In our year in Barcelona, we became big fans of a new group from Liverpool, England, the Beatles. I learned where Liverpool was.

We didn't live far from our school. After school Linda would come home with us until her parents would pick her up. I considered Linda my first girlfriend. We would walk in fields behind our apartment and laugh a lot. Helen found a beau whose father was the Pastor of a church in Barcelona. The four of us would go to an amusement park on a mountain called Tibidabo. We would take a funicular up the hill to the park. It is so cool.

Linda was pretty (and still is). Her name appropriately translated to "pretty" in Spanish. I was so proud that she would hang out with me.

We decided that the four of us should go to a restaurant together. My parents approved. We asked Aunt June. She said she would ask Uncle Gerald the next time they spoke. He said, "Absolutely not." I was 13, and Linda was still 12. I suspect the McNeelys didn't want us to think we were dating. Our "relationship" was platonic. I hadn't developed the hormones to want to touch her.

We Continue Planting Churches

Restrictions on protestant churches' worshipping made creating new churches more difficult than it should have been. You could not put out a flyer about a new church or take a survey on which location would be best for a new church. It had to be done quietly with little fanfare.

Churches began in many types of places. People's homes were a good place, but few believers had a house big enough to host very many people. You couldn't move to the backyard because this would draw the attention of the police. Beauty parlors became a popular place. They had chairs and a bit larger room. They still had a limited capacity if the group began to grow. The point was to grow the group until it was too large for the venue and then convince the FMB to buy a location for the church. Renting was impractical because the Catholic church, through the police, put pressure on the landlord to evict the church.

The most unusual location where we fanned the flames of a new church was a chicken coop outside Barcelona. It was behind the believer's home, with a fence around it. The chicken coop no longer held chickens and was cleaned of the waste from the chickens. It had as many folding chairs as it could hold.

A fan helped air circulate. My mother is leading the singing. You can see my Dad singing on the right and preparing to preach. Margaret is on the left in the back (glasses). This appears to hold about 50 people, pretty good for an informal church.

The service is over. My mother seems to be giving informations to some ladies. The man in the middle, Sr. Leon said he was not a big fan of Americans, but he thanked us for beating Hitler. He enjoyed teasing us.

THE KENNEDY ASSASSINATION

The most traumatic event in 1963 was the killing of President Kennedy. It caused huge changes in the world. We had gone to a Friday night movie, "The Man Who Shot Liberty Valance," with John Wayne and Jimmy Stewart.

We returned home at about 8:30 P.M. Our apartment was on the first floor. We had a doorman (called "portero" in Spain) greeting people who came in. He told us, "han assessinado el presidente." We asked him to repeat this and thought he was hysterical. We entered our house and turned our radio on to the BBC. We didn't yet have a TV set. From the radio we heard one example of bad news after another. I went to bed wondering if anybody was safe. Did the Russians do it? Would we have a nuclear war?

None of these questions had good answers. My father assured me that Lyndon Johnson, the new president, was up to the job. I never trusted him. I didn't see the funeral procession on TV. Helen bought every magazine that featured pictures of the Kennedys, of the funeral procession and of the accused assassin. She pasted these pictures into scrapbooks that she kept for years. At the time, I considered myself a Republican. I hoped that Richard Nixon would try again for the presidency. In 1964, I supported Goldwater, the last Republican I have ever supported for President.

Ladies And Gentlemen, The Beatles

There was a big build-up in early 1964 to the appearance of the Beatles on the Ed Sullivan Show. Of course, we didn't see it, but we read all the publicity about them afterward. From knowing nothing, we became familiar with John, Paul, George and Ringo.

Linda brought an EP of the Beatles, with "Love Me Do" and "Twist and Shout." (An EP had twice as many songs on it than a single did). I had not heard harmonies like theirs before and wanted to hear more. The EPs on the Spanish market were 75 pesetas, which was about $1.25. Helen, Margaret and I had an allowance of 25 pesetas. We would pool our money and buy a new EP each week. Record companies in Britain and the US, Parlophone and Capitol, had a surplus of Beatle songs. Because of the incredible demand for their music, they released all of them at once. It was a really dumb marketing strategy but a treasure of new music for us. The three of us bought one EP each weekend for months. We would listen to the songs with Linda.

My mother hoped the Beatles would be a passing fad. After months of hearing us play their records every day, she gave up. We stopped buying Beatle EPs together but never stopped being fans of the "Fab Four."

OUR MUSIC EDUCATION

Margaret, Helen and I enjoyed the Beatles music in part because we had spent years in piano lessons. The Spanish method of teaching piano was called "Solfeo," which is referred to in English as Solfege. It involves teaching the notes by having you sing them before you try to play the notes on the piano. The student also had to direct an imaginary orchestra, moving his hands down, sideways and up. The notes in Spanish might be Do-Do-Sol-Sol-La-La-Sol. That was the tune Twinkle Twinkle Little Star. Later, I enrolled my sons in Suzuki violin. I was less impressed by the same song, with a staccato rhythm and the words "Mississippi Hotdog."

Many people I know hated this teaching method. Later, my brother, John, refused to take piano lessons until my mother found a teacher who didn't use the Solfeo method.

Although I wasn't happy at singing the notes, I discovered that this method shaped my brain and probably led to my skills playing the piano by ear. I learned to play by notes. Solfeo taught me to see the notes in my mind. I could hear a tune and figured out how to play it without notes. Playing by ear kept me from becoming a good pianist playing from notes. It helped me later when I began playing an accordion.

I learned to play the violin in elementary school. I also learned to play the trumpet in high school. My father was an expert on the harmonica. He learned instinctively to cover up some notes with his tongue. He also played the guitar and later a harp. He was better than me on his instruments, and I was better on mine. I had a good ear for quality piano playing, and I never thought my playing was all that good. I became a perfectionist who stopped playing because I thought my playing was subpar.

Uncle Joe Brings Me An Accordion

The Meffords were always a year after us for furloughs. We returned to Spain in 1963. The Meffords came back to Spain in 1964. The Meffords had lived at a mission home on "easy street" in Yazoo city. The Whittens later stayed at the house. Both families learned that despite the home address, there was no "easy street" on furlough. It was usually hard work.

Joe Mefford's accordion had broken. When he returned to the US, he mentioned his need for a new one. Generous Baptists gave him two. The accordions probably came from a church "love offering," which came from passing a collection plate for a specific gift. Joe Mefford brought both accordions back to Spain and gave me one. He came to our home with a large package and a sly grin. I couldn't believe it!

My accordion had a keyboard on the right and 80 Bass buttons on the left side. It had levers on the right side that made it sound like an organ, a clarinet and other musical instrument. It was an electronic piano before such things existed, operating on wind drawn through when you pulled it out and back.

The keys were shiny, pearly white. The rest of the accordion was a deep, shiny black. It was beautiful. You played it sideways with a braille technique. You could only feel the buttons and the keyboard. I didn't know any other kid with an accordion like mine. Playing it got me a lot of compliments.

When Uncle Joe and I were in the same place, we played accordion duets. We played together at camps. At Christmas time, I would take the accordion to play for caroling. You couldn't play the accordion with mittens. Sometimes, I would play in bone jarring cold, with my fingers going numb. It was worth it to appear cool to my peers, including pretty girls. I later learned that the accordion was not considered cool anymore and was mocked by many. By then, I had learned other ways to be cool.

Madrid From 1964-1965

With the Meffords back in Spain, we moved to Madrid. We found a house to rent not far from the home we had from 1959-1962. I started High school at the military dependents' school on the base at Torrejon. Helen was in 10th grade.

We moved into a home on Francisco De Goya. It had three floors. The yard was paved. It had a shed in the back that had three rooms in it. Rita lived on the bottom floor. I was on the middle floor. I had a quarter bath near my bedroom. I felt a great sense of independence. Margaret stayed in the bottom floor near Rita for a while but decided to move upstairs into a room with Helen. John had his own room, in between the girls' room and the parents' room.

Our house offered a lot for me. When I entered high school, I was the only boy in a typing class. I learned how to type and got my parents to buy me an upright typewriter. Few people today know the thrill of typing on a manual typewriter, hitting the return lever when it reached its limit on the right and the clacking of the keys. More on this later.

Our Seat. Our house at Francisco de Goya is behind the car

THE SUMMER OF 1964 WAS EVENTFUL

After we set up our house, we had big trips to take in the summer. The first was to the seminary in Rushlikon for a regional missionary meeting. My father sang a solo at a meeting. My friends complimented me on his singing voice. We MKs enjoyed getting to know an increasing number of friends from places like Germany and France.

We had another missionary couple assigned to Spain at the conference, Tom and Betty Law. They had been served in Cuba and had escaped Castro's arrival on one of the last flights out of Havana. The elder Tom was a flamboyant man. He wrapped the family dog in his formal raincoat and carried her secretly on the flight with them. He was not afraid to express an opinion. At meetings with Spanish Baptists, he didn't complain when the pastors smoked. He would open up a window and stick his head out, coughing theatrically. We loved the Laws.

The law had four sons, Tommie (my age), Dickie (Margaret's age), Charlie and Stevie (John's age). As they got older, the names became Tom III, Richard, Charles and Stephen. They became great friends to all of us.

From Switzerland, we went through Germany. We were intrigued by Berlin, which at the time was still divided. We went through "Checkpoint Charley." It was a slow time there, and we managed to travel through it into East Berlin. This checkpoint was a part of the infamous wall that the East Germans had built to prevent their citizens from escaping to the West.

Beyond the wall into East Berlin, the buildings had not been repaired after the bombing in World War II. There were few people walking around there. We stopped at a store and bought a loaf of bread, which I recall was hard and tasteless. East Berlin, as we saw it was a sad place.

From Germany, we went to Amsterdam next. It was the site for an International Baptist convention. Most of the missionaries who attended the conference stayed in modest hotels and ate in inexpensive restaurants. My father had purchased a tent in the US that was big enough for the six of us. We used it to save the mission board money.

It had been raining in Amsterdam for days. The camping site in which we had reservations only had a spot that was very wet. My dad had found a large piece of plastic that was discarded. He hoped to use it to keep the bottom of our tent trying. No such luck. The only place where we felt dry was at the convention building.

When the convention dismissed for the day, we went to the house where Ann Frank had hidden. It was several stories high but not very deep. The space in which the Frank family hid was cramped, to say the least. Seeing this made the Diary of Ann Frank more vivid to us.

WE HEARD MARTIN LUTHER KING, JR. PREACH

The most memorable part of our trip wasn't the sights or food. Martin Luther King, Jr. was on his way to Stockholm to collect a Nobel Peace Prize awarded to him in 1964. On the way he stopped in Amsterdam to make the keynote speech at our conference.

Over the years of hearing my father and other preachers in English and Spanish. I can say that I became somewhat of an expert on preachers. My father was a very good preacher. I saw Billy Graham preach on TV and did a simultaneous translation of one of his sermons from English to Spanish. I have even heard the legendary preacher R.G. Lee in his sermon "Payday Someday." (It's a modern-day version of "Sinners in the Hands of an Angry God" by Jonathan Edwards).

MLK was by far the best preacher I ever heard. We bought a book of his sermons. Usually, a written sermon is pretty dry. His were as compelling on paper as they were when he delivered them.

I later learned how down-to-earth Martin Luther King was. Before he came to Amsterdam, he passed through Madrid. A worker at the American embassy heard rumors that MLK was in town. He didn't know what hotel he was at. This worker, named Michael Aaron Rockland, got the assignment to help an American in distress at a hotel. He knocked on the hotel, and MLK answered it in his boxer shorts. He was suffering from diarrhea. Rockland got him a Spanish over-the-counter medicine.

Rockland wrote about his experiences with MLK in a book titled "An American Diplomat in Franco's Spain." He took MLK on a tour of Madrid. Rockland, who was Jewish, saw parallels between the sufferings of Jews in Russia and current civil rights atrocities in the American South. Rockland said he did not have much hope that racial harmony would come to the United States. MLK told him not to give up! Rockland marveled that MLK was traveling alone.

Creating A Camp At Denia

In the early 1960s, the Spanish mission made plans to create a camp in South Spain for youth worship and any other large meetings the Spanish Baptist convention wanted to schedule. There was a strong church in a town called Denia, which was not far from some very nice beaches. The Pastor of the church there, Joaquin Pastor, had been a friend since we arrived in 1953.

The FMB sent money to buy the property. When we left on furlough, Joe Mefford was left in charge of beginning the development of the project. I think my parents expected to return to find small buildings, to house campers and to cook food for them.

My parents were shocked in 1963 to discover Joe Mefford had spent almost all the money on an Olympic-sized swimming pool! It was beautiful and was a good reason for people to come to a camp in Denia. Where would they sleep and go to the bathroom? Where would the camp store food for large groups of campers?

My parents were beside themselves!

The swimming pool in 1964

The situation was not quite as bad as my parents saw it initially. More money was appropriated for a building (on the lower right of the picture). It had the only bathroom on the property. It had a kitchen with refrigerator space. It also had space for campers who didn't want to sleep in outside tents to use their sleeping bags on the floor.

Spanish people were not expecting luxury at a camp (an indoor bed being one of those luxuries). They had grown up sleeping outdoors. Cooking over a campfire was familiar to them. Getting around by the light of flashlights was OK too.

Denia already had an incredible luxury, the massive swimming pool. It became one of the main attractions for coming to camp and still is. The swimming pool, which could have been called Joe Mefford's folly, became Joe Mefford's genius.

The pool a couple of years later. You can see the campers. In the background you can see Denia, and the Mediterranean.

The campground was an adventure. The ground was tough and rocky. Most of the trees were Algaroba (carob) and produced a fruit I refused to eat. Some people say that in the Bible, this fruit was fed to pigs and that the Prodigal Son, at his worst moment, ate them too. Ground up, they can have medicinal benefits.

The Denia beach was not very good. The town of Denia was a great place to relax. When were weren't working at the camp, Uncle Joe would take us to a cafe to drink Granisados de Lemon, a Lemonade slushie. Sitting outside, we watched tourists embarrass themselves. This was the era of the "Ugly American," tourists with a lot of money who had no cultural sensitivity. They made no secret that they felt superior to Spanish people. My goal each day that I lived in Spain was to show my Spanish friends I was not one of those Americans.

Outdoor Movies

There was no enclosed movie theater in Denia. A business with a large space with a fence around it would project a movie on a screen. The viewers would sit on small straw chairs to watch. At night, gentle breezes blew across us. I enjoyed watching movies this way.

Do It Yourself Bullfights

One of the most unusual Denia attractions was a makeshift opportunity for young men to pretend to be a bullfighter. The bulls were young and not trained to charge a cape. The city set out a half stadium, with the open side emptying into the sea. Young men often stoked their courage with alcoholic beverages with homemade capes. They didn't have any weapons to use against the bulls. When one approached them, the men would jump into the smelly sea. Even a small bull could trample you, causing serious injury. It was all drunk fun for the participants. I had no desire to join them.

I prided myself in my cultural understanding of Spain. I never had any sympathy for real bullfighting. I saw it as torturing and killing an animal that was taught to be aggressive, similar in many ways to cockfighting. In comparison to Christians and Lions in the Roman Coliseum, the Bulls were the Christians. Bullfighting is on the wane now. The Catalonia province has banned it.

Going To School On Torrejon AFB

In the two years we were gone from Madrid, the Air Force had consolidated all the schools at Torrejon AFB and at Royal Oaks, a housing project for military and their dependents. Margaret was assigned to the Royal Oaks, and Helen and I took the high school on the base.

I took typing, which turned out to be one of the most practical courses I had in high school. I also took a class in German. The first thing the teacher taught us was parts of speech. Depending upon the person talking and other context, you had different words for the word "the." It was not a conversational German course. I passed it but learned very little actual German.

We had a history teacher who told us the current leaders of Germany were weak and the country would probably return to fascism. If we had a greater knowledge of history at age 13, we would have found this alarming.

My memory of high school teachers in my freshman year was that several of them were weird looking. I formed a theory that the higher up you got in school, from high school to college, the stranger the teachers looked and behaved.

My First Experience In Denia

In the summer of 1965, my mother, Lila Mefford and June McNeely were in charge of a young girl's camp. Most of the girls slept in the large building across from the swimming. We brought our tent and pitched it up the hill from the swimming pool on a flat space under a large tree. All the Whitten kids were there. My father had business appointments. The tent was easy to put up. There are all the positives about sleeping in a tent.

My air mattress deflated often, usually when I was asleep. I was heard many nights pumping the air mattress. Even using a sleeping bag under me, with the air mattress keeping me off the ground, I had problems going to sleep. It was hot in the tent. It was even less fun when it rained. It was also boring. It was no match for a Holiday Inn.

Aunt June had some misgivings about having a 13-year-old boy around so many girls. She kept an eagle eye on me. I played the accordion for worship services.

To my right is Aunt Lila Mefford

This was a typical worship service at camp in 1965.

At the end of the camp, Aunt June pronounced me a "perfect gentleman." Fifty years later, Aunt June wrote a book about her experiences as a missionary titled "Called Step by Step." She mentioned that she promised me a coke if I behaved myself. It took four years for me to collect on this promise.

After reading "Step by Step" I wondered if we had been in the same country as the McNeelys. Aunt June portrayed Spain as a lot more difficult country to live in than I remembered it. I guess it's all from your point of view.

Helping Cubans

My office space in the back building at our house was affected by an inflow of Cuban refugees in Madrid in 1965. Wealthy and religious Cubans complained about Castro from New Year's Day 1959 when Castro had taken over the country. Their efforts led to a disastrous invasion of Cuba, called the "Bay of Pigs" in 1961, Castro's opposition included his older sister, who was prominent in the Cuban Baptist church. Eventually, she fled the country, along with many Cubans. In 1965 Castro gave Cubans who wanted to leave the opportunity to leave legally.

The catch was that they could only take the clothes they were carrying and what they could hold. Most Cubans wanted to go to Miami, which was 90 miles away from Havana. This was too close for Castro's comfort. He sent the refugees to prominent countries that would accept them, Spain, Mexico and Colombia.

Some of the Cuban refugees were Baptist. They looked to us for help. We helped more than the Baptists. The Spanish government provided a temporary place for them to live. We collected clothing and other supplies they would need. Those who had not stashed money outside Cuba were penniless. The supplies took over all three rooms in the back of our property, temporarily displacing me from my office.

I didn't mind. I had a fondness for the Cuban people and a lifelong dislike of Fidel Castro. A popular song of the time said, "When I left

Cuba, I left my heart buried there." I still have an emotional response to it.

Those Cubans who came through Madrid were usually highly educated and right-wing. In late 1967, I traveled on a train to a youth convention in south Spain with a middle-aged Cuban. She argued that MLK was a communist. I disagreed strongly.

The Cubans who came by our home appreciated our help appreciated it. In 1966, they gave a dinner for us in our backyard, with chicken, black beans and other elements of Cuban cuisine. Thirty years later, my parents stopped in Miami after showing me Argentina. The Cubans in Miami honored them with another dinner.

What Nationality Was I?

Around the age of 15, I began to ponder this question. My first nationality was American. I had a birth certificate issued by the US State Department proving this. I also had a birth certificate issued by Argentine authorities. My connection to Argentina seemed theoretical at the time. I wasn't eligible to be a citizen by birth in Spain. Margaret and John were. I found myself bristling when Spanish people criticized the USA.; I could criticize my own country, but they couldn't. When people in Mississippi mocked Spain, I would chalk it up to racism and xenophobia.

Although I had no citizenship in Spain, I had a lot of emotional ties there. Every time Spain lost an international tournament, soccer, tennis or the Eurovision Song competition, I hurt along with the Spanish people. When the World Cup came around in Soccer, I rooted for both Spain and Argentina. Thankfully, the two never met in the World Cup.

Which country did I like the best? I liked them both. As I considered my becoming an adult in the next three years, which country would I live in as my forever home? Probably neither. If I had money, I would probably have a home in both countries. I looked forward to a life of travel, discoveries and personal growth.

Coming To Term With My Mississippi Roots

I loved my grandparents and my other relatives in Mississippi. I didn't love Mississippi. Their reputation was terrible in the 1960s. Just before we left in 1963, the director of the NAACP, a black man named Medgar Evers in Jackson. The assassin was not brought to justice in the 1960s. Three civil rights workers were kidnapped and murdered in the county adjacent to my grandparents. The murderers were pictured chewing tobacco and joking at their trial. A Mississippi jury would not convict a white man for killing a black man in the 1960s. These atrocities were going on all over the South.

I returned to Spain with an aversion to anybody with a southern accent. My parents softened their accents in years of international work. The US military had a disproportionate group of people from the American South, both black and white.

I should not have stereotyped servicemen by their accents. I had a good reason to criticize some of them, the ones who were not happy to be outside the United States. Uncle Sam had given them an incredible opportunity to get to know another culture, and they didn't take advantage of it. They could have taken their huge American cars, some twice the size of our Seat, and traveled north of Madrid to see castles at Segovia or the walled city of Toledo, where you could buy inlaid Toledo Gold jewelry and see paintings by El Greco and the studio where he painted them in the 1500s.

They could have headed south to an area called La Mancha, the place where Miguel Cervantes set his book "Don Quixote. There were great beaches on the coast of Spain. With all these cultural riches, including a world-famous art museum, The Prado, they chose to stay on the base at Torrejon or at Royal Oaks, buying their groceries at the PX and seeing American movies at the base movie theater. What a waste!

It took years of observing people like my Uncle Bruce to change the stereotype of Southerners. My mother's younger brother was actually Earl Bruce Mitchell, Ph.D. in entomology. He was a professor at Mississippi State University, doing research on the boll weevil. This insect did considerable damage to cotton crops. His wife, Sue Mitchell, had a Ph.D. in education. Bruce was a friend to the international students at Mississippi State. When Bruce got home from work and took his boots off, he would read letters from the students who had returned to their country, usually thanking him for his support while they were in the US.

The youngest of the Mitchell siblings, Henry Cooper Mitchell, always called HC, also had a Ph.D. in entomology. He worked with Bruce on research. Bruce and H.C. were a sight together! I later considered them the Blues Brothers of Mississippi entomology.

The openness of the Bruce Mitchells was shown when their oldest child, Judy, came to Spain to visit us a couple of times. She met Josh Weiner at a camp in upstate New York and, after a tumultuous courtship, married him. Josh is Jewish. I did not hear any hint of objections by Bruce or Sue to Judy's marrying outside her family's religion. Judy and Josh both have law degrees and have practiced law in Jackson for decades.

I was wrong to stereotype Mississippians. I still have no desire to live in Mississippi. I have a son who is disabled and black. I don't want him to experience any more racism than possible. I still believe the politicians who run Mississippi, all Democrats until the 70s and all Republicans afterward, are not doing the best for their constituents.

Mississippi has the lowest income, the poorest education, the poorest health and so on. It seems to go on and on.

My Uncle H. C. was exposed to toxic chemicals and died of cancer in the late 70s. In retirement, Uncle Bruce had a lot of fun. He introduced catfish into the pond on his farm in order to have a place for the family to fish. When otters began eating the catfish, he brought in goats to go after the otters. In order to make the goats comfortable, he built a two-story goat house for them.

Bruce built a one-hole golf course in his front yard. He also built a swimming pool to the side of his house. His greatest love was entertaining the grandchildren and singing "Milk Cow Blues." He bought a four-wheeler to get around his farm and attached a trailer on the back. When we visited, he would allow the older ones to drive the four-wheeler. He also had ponies for them to ride. My kids thought of Uncle Bruce's farm as Disneyland Louisville.

Becoming More Involved With The Denia Camp

Our family in 1966

1966 had several memorable events. An American bomber accidentally dropped an atomic bomb in the Mediterranean, near the coast of Spain. This was an embarrassing event for the US.

Both the US and Spain tried to keep it quiet. If the bomb gave off radiation, it could do serious damage to the Spanish tourist industry. When the story became public, it drew a lot of media attention.

Going to school on Torrejon Air Force base, we got to see the consequences of military actions involving the USA. In the last two years, the US had expanded the war in Vietnam. We saw many planes coming through, carrying soldiers to or from Vietnam.

We saw many airplanes come through as part of the search for the bomb. There were rumors flying about the progress of the search. Eventually, we learned the bomb was discovered with no radiation damage to Spain. Few people actually believed this.

Early in the summer of 1966 we had the annual mission meeting, this time at the seminary in Barcelona. Mission meetings often seemed like a family reunion. My dad had developed a credible donkey bray in college. At the time of prayer, somebody would say, "Charles Whitten will now bray." The ones who weren't familiar with the joke would bow their heads, and my dad would bray loudly.

The Missionaries in 1966, I don't remember all the names L to R My mother, Betty Law, June McNeely (don't know the lady in white), Lila Mefford, and Mrs Schweinsburg.

Most husbands are behind their wives. Dan and Frieda White are next to my dad; Tom Law is next. Joe Mefford is on the far right.

The mission still didn't pay for childcare. They decided at this meeting that the older MKs would run a Vacation Bible School. It all went well except for a mischievous child named Skipper Bryan. Skipper once fell out of a bed at our house and broke his collarbone. We were not trained in childcare, so we tried a unique way of controlling Skipper. We tied him to his chair. The adults didn't freak out when they learned of this. They advised us not to do that again. Probably, they marked this down as a last straw and made plans to keep the teenagers busy and to have more reliable care for the younger MKs.

TEENAGED GIRLS IN MY HOUSE

Early in the summer, we made plans to attend a camp in Denia. It was another girl's camp, being run by my missionary aunts. Aunt Lila and my mother were present, but Aunt June was not.

Two girls were brought to Madrid from a town in north Spain, Renteria. There was no place arranged for them to stay, so we put them up on cots in our living room. I liked their looks, although I didn't get to talk to them yet. I only remember the name of one, Esther Sampedro.

There were two cute girls on cots a few feet from my bedroom. I didn't know what to do about it, so I did nothing. Nothing is often the best to do when you are uncertain.

Tony Mefford was also present at the camp. I had borrowed a trombone from the beginner's band. I had my trumpet. Each day, when it was time for the campers to get up, we would play our instruments in the tune that wakes up military trainees.

The girls from Renteria felt like their staying at our home made us old friends. We talked a lot at the camp. When it was over, I got their address, and we became pen pals. Some people in my family thought that I had a girlfriend at last, but this was not to be.

In the summer of 1966, there was another missionary conference at Ruschlikon. Because we teenagers had participated in some shenanigans in the past, the organizers of the organizers decided to send the teenage MKs to a ski camp in the mountains of Switzerland.

The arrow points to where we slept. This picture comes from a postcard that I wrote but didn't send to Esther Sampedro.

I called this building a camp rather than a resort because it wasn't a luxury accommodation. Being in the summer, there was no snow around it. There were about twenty-five MKs from Spain, Italy, Germany and Austria. There were people there who cleaned and cooked. There were a couple of young adults running the program.

The person in charge was a stout German woman who spoke very little English. We nicknamed her "Frau Governess." The programming was OK. The food was not. It was basic working-class German cuisine, wiener schnitzel, vegetables, hard bread and unsweet chocolate. One reason Frau Governess may have pretended to know little English was to not have to deal with our complaints.

Dick Law had a birthday. Helen, Janie and Linda McNeely approached the cooks to explain that in the US, we celebrate a birthday with a cake. They had no cake mixes, but the girls knew how to make a cake from scratch. We praised the cooks. It was the best thing we had eaten all week.

You might think we had a miserable time. Quite the contrary — we had the time of our lives. Being isolated in the mountains meant that Frau Governess couldn't report back to our parents, and there were very few consequences we had to suffer. Most of the other MKs were old friends, so we had a great time.

Tony Mefford had returned after his first year in college. All of the other boys were in awe of him. Janie had assured us that Tony had many girlfriends, and they were gorgeous and shapely. Tony told us stories about his experiences with girls, stopping short of describing his conquests. We younger boys were scandalized and yet in wonder. Actually, we had no idea what he was talking about.

Tony Smoked Cigarettes. This Was Forbidden By Frau

Governess. Tony would sneak out of our room at night to smoke. Frau Governess. The portly Frau vowed to catch him in the act. We younger boys had decided that Tony was laughing at our expense, so we decided to play a prank on him. When he was out of the room, we short-sheeted his bed.

After his nightly cigarette, Tony ran into our room, which was actually a barracks, just a few minutes ahead of the Frau. He took his pants off and tried to get under his sheet so he could claim to have been there all along. His legs would only go so far. As the Frau entered our room, he was outside his bed, with his underwear showing. We thought this was funny. Probably not him.

A student missionary was leading the spiritual part of the camp. We divided up into groups.

My group. The other boy was named Craighead, an MK from Italy. Linda McNeely was on the far right.

Each group was asked to write a Christian chorus. I wrote a forgettable one. I remember it, but it was not very good.

1967 - Helen Graduates And I Become "El Judio"

In 1967, I had John Morris as my English teacher for the third year in a row. His approach to teaching was lackadaisical. He rarely lectured us. He didn't have a textbook. The students in his class were supposed to write anything they wanted, an essay, poem, etc. and turn it in to him. He would read it over and return it with comments. At the end of a grading period, he called you to his desk and asked what grade you deserved. This was no time for modesty. If you wanted an A but thought you deserved a B, you got the B. Had you asked for an A, you would have received it. I always asked for an A.

I wasn't into fiction. I wrote him a series of short essays on what was wrong with the world. He announced to the class that I was the biggest rebel in the class. I wasn't sure why he said this, but at least he noticed me.

Mr. Morris' method had some problems for students - we didn't learn about punctuation, vocabulary, writing techniques and so forth. I liked this method because it allowed me independent study in the library at any time that I wanted. Mr. Morris' method came from a book called "Summerhill" by A.S. Neill. Neill was a believer in the philosophy of the French philosopher Rousseau. Rosseau wrote that man was inherently good. It was the constrictions of society that led to evil.

The students at Summerhill were given the freedom to do whatever they wanted in class. In addition to Rousseau, Neill was a follower of Freud. When a child misbehaved in class, Neill believed that it was because he wondered where babies came from. Neill would tell him, and the bad behavior would stop.

I read Summerhill and was impressed by it at first. It took me years to decide that Rousseau, Neill and Freud did not jell. This educational philosophy was, at best, "Simplistic" and, at worst, "bullshit." I put the word simplistic in quotes because everyone now uses it when they mean "simple." It does not. I have given up on trying to educate people on this.

Mr. Morris was convinced that in addition to being a rebel, I was also smart. One day he stopped me in the hallway and asked for the meaning of "iconoclast." A student had used this word in class, and Morris didn't want to admit that he didn't know the meaning. I wondered why Morris didn't have a dictionary in his classroom. I knew the meaning - it's a person who tries to smash other people's most cherished beliefs, their icons.

Morris didn't tell us where babies come from. We all knew. His class worked for me because I was an independent learner.

One year, I was on independent studies for English, Spanish and History. Most of my classmates did not share my reading habits or my push to learn.

My Readings

I read everything that was published in Reader's Digest. Each month, the published a condensed book. If it was interesting, I would get the whole book. I got books from the school library. I also checked books out of the USIS library that were sponsored through the Embassy. I read How to Make Friends and Influence People by Dale

Carnegie. I was a shy young man and wanted to know the answer. I didn't make any more friends after I read the book, but I learned some basic lessons about human nature. Carnegie said that everyone thought of himself as a good guy, whether it was Billy Graham or Al Capone. There was no point in trying to change their mind or to win an argument with anybody.

I loved Catch 22 by Joseph Heller. It was funny and tragic. Although it was fiction, some of the craziness shown in the hierarchy of the military was evident on the base where I was going to school. I swore that I would never serve in the military.

My friend, Dan Neely, introduced me to Ayn Rand. She was an atheist born in Russia. Her novels, including "Atlas Shrugged," preached that everyone was selfish. Altruism was a myth that prevented capitalism from reaching its true strength in America. This ran contrary to what I had learned in church, so I eventually rejected it.

I read 1984 and Animal Farm by George Orwell and Brave New World by Aldous Huxley. I found both writers fascinating and looked up more books by them.

As I grew older, I made a mental list of people that I admired. The first person on this list was Jesus. As I got to know Him better, my admiration grew. Most of my heroes were people with the same issues as me, who had human flaws.

Human heroes did admirable things without making a big deal about it. When you praise them, they would change the subject. They didn't do what they did for praise. Paul Newman was one of my favorite actors. He created a line of salad dressings and spaghetti sauces. These items sold because of his celebrity. He raised more than $100 million and gave it all to a camp for disabled children. If asked about his generosity, he would say that others deserved more credit than him, usually telling a joke on himself. My parents were like that.

Albert Schweitzer was born on the same day as me, January 14. He was a theologian and an accomplished organ player, performing Bach on the massive organs at major cathedrals in Europe. He also knew how to fix the organs. In his early 40s, he decided to become a country doctor in Africa. When he applied to enter the medical school at the same university where he taught theology, his colleagues suggested that his first entry exam should be a psychiatric test! He became a doctor in the country of Gabon, not far from where my parents served their last years before retiring as Missionaries. When people said I was crazy to adopt so many kids, I thought of Albert Schweitzer.

My heroes included Martin Luther King, Jr. and Mahatma Gandi. Both were assassinated. Both made a difference in their times. I also admired William Wilberforce, the British prime minister in the early 1800s who persisted over decades of resistance to end the trafficking of human beings from Africa. His life and his family reminded me of another politician I admired. Robert Kennedy, Sr.

I admired teachers who had an important part in my development, Oakley P. McEachren in high school, Dr. Joe Cooper in college, and Dr. Brent Wiliams in graduate school.

I wanted recognition for my achievements. When it came, it made me feel embarrassed and undeserving. My lifetime achievements are on the backs of people who came before me and two wonderful Christian women that I married.

Our Trip To Paris

Helen graduated from high school in 1967, and made plans to enroll in Mississippi college in the fall. My parents asked her what she wanted for a graduation gift. She chose a trip to the Holy Land. Unfortunately, the Six Days War made this impossible, so she had to try again. She chose Paris.

We took in the sights from Paris. I climbed the Eiffel Tower.

We saw Picasso's paintings in the Louvre Museum. Spain's Prado Museum was as good as the Louvre. It did not have Picasso because Picasso hated Franco. One of Picasso's most famous paintings was titled "Guernica." It was an abstract depiction of fascist bombings in Spain during the Spanish Civil War. After Franco died, Picasso allowed his sculptures and paintings to return to Spain in a museum dedicated to him, the Reina Sofia Museum.

The most incredible thing we saw in Paris was not a building or a painting. We entered a French record shop and saw an album with what looked like a painting on it. It was the Beatles' "Sgt Pepper's Lonely Hearts Club Band." We wanted to buy it but had no money.

Less than a year earlier, John Lennon had declared that the Beatles were more popular than Jesus. This caused an incredible controversy, including the burning of Beatles albums. My parents wanted us to get rid of all our Beatle records. We said that "popular" didn't mean "better" and that this was only John Lennon's opinion. We compromised by agreeing to turn the Beatles off if they had any Baptist bigwigs over at our house. We also managed to get my dad to buy Sgt Peppers for us.

Years later, when I was a father, my Dad admitted to me that he really liked some of the Beatle's songs. I told him that I liked many songs by Frank Sinatra, more songs than I liked by Elvis. I probably should have mentioned Bing Crosby, but the only song I could remember at the time by Crosby was "White Christmas."

My Summer In Denia As "El Judio"

In 1967 the attendance at Denia camp had grown dramatically. The Mission Board had paid for a two-story building that had rooms for the campers to sleep. There was a large kitchen and dining room on the first floor. With tables taken out it doubled as a meeting room.

With a record attendance expected, Uncle Joe tried to meet the needs of the campers. The campers were a brisk walk away from Denia. The campers wanted to be able to buy snacks in their free time. It was impractical to accompany a large group of campers on a snack trip and then supervise them in their purchases. It was even less practical to allow groups to go on their own. Uncle Joe asked me to stay at the camp all summer long, running a small store. He said I could keep the profits. I agreed.

I was willing to do this for several reasons. I loved the camp and welcomed the opportunity to meet campers of all ages from all parts of Spain. I was OK with a small job that made me some money.

There was a small shed in the middle of the camp used to store tools and cleaning supplies. I set up a table inside it. I bought postcards and stamps, chocolates, salted sunflower seeds, and bubble gum. I also bought drinks and ice. Uncle Joe painted the words "El Rastro" over the front door of the shed. A rastro was a flea market, an apt name for my business. My business plan was simple: I doubled the price of what I had paid for my supplies.

My prices turned out to be controversial. Since we were in a Christian camp, some campers thought I should sell my wares for what I paid for them. I patiently explained that Spain was a capitalist country. I had no reason to spend hours buying supplies, preparing them to sell and then waiting on them when for nothing, no matter how pretty the girls were.

I was quickly dubbed "El Judio." Of course, this is Spanish for the Jew. Years later, this antisemitic slur bothered me. Jewish people liked to make money. So did Christians and Muslims.

I wasn't the only MK who spent the whole summer at the camp. We had purchased the Beatles album "Sgt Peppers Lonely Hearts Club Band." Janey Mefford had received the first album of the Doors through the mail. Its biggest hit was "Light My Fire." All the other songs were good. We spent a lot of time in her room, listening to this album on her record player.

1967 was the last time I stayed at the Camp in Denia. I have many wonderful memories there. Camping at Denia declined over the next decades. The Baptist Church at Denia, led by my old friend, Jorge Pastor, converted it into a Christian school. Here is a picture of a recent enrollment:

Class of 2024, Denia

The Denia, where I met many Spanish friends, where I sold goods under the nickname "El Judio" as a teenager, is long gone.

It remains fresh in my memories.

Coming Out Of My Cocoon In My Senior Year

The school and the base added a dorm for students whose parents were civilians and whose jobs didn't allow them to take kids with them. This had businessmen who couldn't take their kids with them to places like Africa, to journalists and to people working at hot spots around the world who wanted their kids close enough that they could visit with them on a break from the jobs.

These students weren't happy to be separated from their families. They also weren't happy to be under the control of people who were a lot stricter on them than their parents had been. They were also very smart. I remember two people from this group, a tall blonde fellow named Mark Singer and a black-haired young woman named Nikki Szulc. I never learned about Mark's parents. Nikki's father was Tad Szulc, a correspondent for the New York Times. They were some of my new friends.

For three years of high school, I had been shy young, many in the out-group. I brought my lunch in a bag and at by myself in the cafeteria. I had friends in the chess club. I didn't go to football games or to school dances. I was a Baptist. We don't dance. To nobody's surprise, I didn't have a girlfriend. I had experienced a crush but didn't have the nerve to approach the girl.

In the spring of 1967, I decided to change, to become more involved in social activities. My first step was to run for office in the upcoming senior class. Because I wasn't well known I decided to forego President or Vice-President. Secretary was considered a girl's job, so that left me with Treasurer. My father was the mission treasurer. Of course, none of these jobs had set duties or powers.

One of the new missionaries, James Buie, had introduced me to a medium called "chalk talk." He would sing a hymn while making a religious drawing that was the subject of his song. I asked him to make posters for my candidacy.

James Buie made funny caricatures of me holding bags of money. My slogans were "Save with Dave" and "Your Money is Safe with Dave." The posters were different from other students' posters. Usually, their poster said, "Vote for Bob for Senior Vice-President." That was plain, to the point, and boring. If the student wanted to be a little risqué, it would have the word SEX in giant letters. Then it would say, "Now that I've got your attention, vote for Bob for Senior Vice President." That tactic was so used that it didn't draw attention anymore. My posters got me the recognition that I lacked.

We had a meeting of the class at the auditorium. I had two opponents. The first one was preppy and entitled. He told the audience that he was already the winner because he was head and shoulders better than the others. That arrogance lost the election for him.

The second candidate was Dan Neely. He was a big fan of Ayn Rand and her philosophy. He was a zany individual. Later, Zany became "schizophrenic." He had been a friend of mine for several years, a fellow member of the out-group. Dan's speech was mostly a summary of an article by Woody Allen in Playboy. He said that everyone had a belly button that fell into one of two categories, either an inny or an outie. Hearing this now, you may wonder why a sophisticated audience found this funny. Of course, my class was not sophisticated at all. They laughed very hard.

Of course, belly laughs didn't guarantee votes. To begin my speech, I said, "I don't think I can top that!" I got almost as many laughs as Dan had. I had read about efforts across the US to exercise "student power." I said my goal was to increase power for students. They would have an advocate when they were called before the principal. We would make changes in the constitution of the student body to give us more rights. Of course, it was unlikely I could achieve these goals, but I was idealistic and thought I could find a way.

I got a nice applause. On the way back to my seat, I caught the eye of Nikki. She was sitting with other girls. I heard her say to them, "Vote for David." That boosted my spirits. I won with 50% of the votes. The other two split the rest evenly. This was the high point of my life up to then!

These were the officers of my class. Of the four I was the only "reform" candidate.

My election as Senior class treasurer said to me that people liked me. It boosted me into the In-crowd. I discovered that although I wasn't being accepted into an exclusive club, I had a door opened for me to hang out with the cool members of my class, the officers, the beautiful people and those who were popular. I was an officer of a class but otherwise didn't actually fit into the categories above.

I got invited to go clubbing with my friends on weekends. I had two small problems, I didn't have a girlfriend, and I didn't know how to dance. As each of my friends danced with the partner they brought, I was single. I didn't know how to dance, and when I tried to dance, I embarrassed myself. Still, I tried to fit in.

I was a class officer, but I wasn't a part of the student council. I fixed this problem by persuading my friends at the chess club to vote for me as their representative in the student council. At a student council meeting, I persuaded a majority to create a Constitution Committee. I was on the committee, as were many of my friends.

This picture has many of my new friends from my senior year

As part of my transformation, I moved from glasses to contact lenses. I would have probably been more popular if I had combed my hair better. I had pimples too. I was at least one year younger than all of the seniors on this picture.

The last of my yearbook pictures. Note Lidia Visbeek, Lindsay Tunnell and Linda Woodring.

My school was created for military dependents. They had enough space left over in classes that they could enroll children of civilians for a not insignificant amount of money. Most of my fellow officers of the senior class and my friends were civilians.

My best friend, Pat Graff, was the son of a writer who was a higher-up in the Mormon Church. Nikki Szulc was the daughter of Tad Szulc, a correspondent for the New York Times. He had revealed the invasion of Cuba, known as the "Bay of Pigs," and had earned the wrath of the Kennedy administration at the time. Tad Szulc emigrated from Poland to Brazil in World War II. Nikki was born in Brazil. I have kept up with Nikki, and have a standing agreement to meet her in Havana when Cuba kicks out the communist party. So far, that hasn't happened.

Breaking my streak of non-involvement with girls, I took two girls out on a date in my senior year, Colleen Fahey and Lidia Visbeek. (they are pictured above). I had known Colleen since 6th grade. I didn't know Lidia before I met her in school. Her parents had attended a Baptist church in Argentina. I never got around to asking her how they came to move to Spain. I didn't know what interested a girl at that age, so I had only one date with both and no goodnight kiss. I would have asked out Nikki Szulc, but she was going with Mark Singer most of the year.

I had a lot of fun with my best friend, Pat Graff. We both came from religious families. The Baptists had substantial differences from the Mormons. We never discussed religion. Pat's father was a screenwriter. He recommended movies to us, and we skipped school to go to those movies. I think we played hooky (skipped school for Gen Zs) for almost a quarter of the year. We were both on independent study, so our teachers didn't miss our absences. We each had a high enough grade point average that we were going to graduate no matter what.

Pat and I took over the morning announcements on the school's intercom. These were announcements on school activities, forms that parents needed to sign and the principal's current warnings to students. We often opened up the announcement with "This is Pat and Dave with the boring, censored news." The Principal didn't mind, mostly because we had turned off his speaker. The teachers didn't turn us in. Occasionally, we would single out a student for mention. We announced that all the Juniors, and Paul Amiel are asked to turn in a certain paper. Margaret was in his class and said he almost jumped out of his skin when his name was mentioned.

The senior class had a concession for candy bars and cokes at the cafeteria. This was to raise money for Senior activities. Pat and I manned the tables. Paul Amiel, the President of the Junior class, had persuaded the student council to give them the drink concession. Maybe this is why we tweaked him in the announcement.

We used the money to finance a Senior class trip to a bull farm known as a Tienta. We hired two buses to take us to the farm. I was in the slower of the buses. The driver had mistaken our instructions and was headed to a town called Atienza. We lost an hour of partying because of this.

Despite this frustration, we had a great time at the bull farm. It had small bulls and alcoholic beverages. The teachers supervising us went to great lengths to make sure that the students did not have any beer. What was to stop the teachers? One of my favorite teachers, Neil Magee, enjoyed some adult beverages, and then was knocked down by a bull, breaking his leg! He came to class with a cast on his leg. The next day, he had a cast on his arm, which had also been broken. He announced that they had 30 seconds and no more to laugh. We lined up to sign his casts. Pat wrote on his arm cast, "Booze and bulls don't mix." Those Mormons could be judgmental.

I had a crush on Linda Collins (pictured above). I never took her out on a date. As I got to know her, I realized that she was addicted to uppers. In her junior year, she had dated a senior who was in college in California. He was murdered while out on a date. This didn't help with her depression. Eventually, she and her family were returned to the US prematurely so that she could get therapy there.

In my senior year, I became a strong supporter of Robert Kennedy, who was running to replace Lyndon Johnson. He did very well, winning a crucial primary in California. On his way out of the hotel where he spoke, he was shot and juked by a Palestinian immigrant. This, combined with the murder of my hero, Martin Luther King, Jr. made me wonder if the USA was out of control.

The killing of RFK Sr. occurred less than a week before we were going to have our high school graduation. President Johnson declared a day of national mourning on the date we were to graduate. I had volunteered to give a speech at the ceremony, and my proposed speech had been approved. All speeches were canceled. My class walked up and received awards and diplomas. At the end of the ceremony, my m. the arching band was to perform an intricate maneuver. The tuba stepped in the wrong direction, and the march fell apart laughing.

RETHINKING MY CHRISTIAN FAITH

As I transitioned to a new David, more gregarious and more popular, I began to wonder about my faith. A preacher like my father represents God. Of course, all fathers should model God. In my case, my father was how I understood God to be. That would be a problem to me at age 17, but a blessing later on in life.

Every child goes through a period of separating from their attachment to their parents, of deciding that when they get independence, they will do things their own way. Some of the separation and move into adult independence is smooth and amicable. Sometimes, the child has to pull away hard to become their own person. This process is essential for each child becoming an adult. If they fail to separate from their parents, they essentially do not grow up.

All this makes sense. The problem for a preacher's son is that if you have to rebel against your father, you are also rebelling against what he has taught you about God. In my 17th year, I decided that everything I believed was spoon-fed to me. Nothing in my beliefs came from what I actually believed. I decided to reboot my beliefs.

I began reading books from a humanist point of view. My reading before had led me to believe in "progress." Each generation, science was making discoveries that improved our lives. Our standard of living was getting better. Our medical advances were increasing our lifespan by 5 years or more every decade. When we set the retirement age at 65 in 1935, we expected it would be at the end of most people's lives. In 1968, the average person was expected to live until at least 80. Human intelligence would make things better for us.

In my optimistic view of the future, I was having a hard time including God. I grew up in a conservative Baptist church, both in the US and Spain. As a child, I saw God as angry and vengeful, impossible to please. We had to tread lightly around him, knowing that we couldn't hide anything from him.

I did not have any guidelines on how to do this change in my thinking. I made the mistake of telling my parents that I considered myself, at least temporarily, to be an agnostic. They freaked out, seeing the failure to see God as the belief that He did not exist. I was looking for proof of God, not proof of non-God.

This caused my parents a lot of pain, which I regretted.

When you rebel, one of the first points is, "I don't want you to tell me what to do." My first act of rebellion was to go to a different Baptist church than my parents did. That would put me out of their control. I usually went to Immanuel. If the sermon bored me, I would cross the street from Immanuel to a cafe to have an expresso. A black expresso coffee can take 15 minutes or more to drink, it's so strong and bitter! I thought about drinking a beer, but I didn't like the taste of beer. Attending a Baptist college taught me how to drink and curse.

The church was the ultimate in telling me what to do and think. I did not attend church very often for more than 10 years. It took a Godly wife and anticipation of being a father to cause me to return to my original faith.

Why did I go through this torturous process when, eventually, I would return to almost where I started from? I was moving toward being a political liberal. I returned to the faith as an evangelical kind of conservative. I believe that Jesus died for our sins and that if we accept Him as our savior, we will someday join Him in heaven. I have concerns about Hell as it is described. I believe women should be leaders in the church.

I started the process in order to be intellectually and spiritually honest. I could not accept other people's beliefs, even if they came from the most reliable people I knew, my parents. My beliefs and my commitments had to be my own. My motives may have been understandable for someone my age, but I talked about it too much. I could have done it better.

Rebellion is the original sin. I certainly committed that sin many times. My return to my faith was delayed by my rebellion. Eventually, I realized that the only way was through Jesus, the way, the truth and the life. I took His way.

GOING TO BERNE, SWITZERLAND

Even though I didn't attend church often, I was willing to go to a Youth conference. In June 1968, I joined a motley crew to go to a Baptist youth conference in Berne, Switzerland. An airman from Torrejon with a nine-passenger station wagon took us. In the car, we had some Spanish youth, airmen from the base, and Tommy Law, a fellow MK.

It was a fun group. Spanish girls have several middle names. We had one girl whose name was Maria Juana. When we approached a border checkpoint, one of the guys would say, "Esconde la Maria Juana." This translates easily into English. In both languages, Mary Jane and Maria-Juana come to the same word, marijuana. Of course, we weren't carrying drugs to a Youth Conference.

One of the airmen had a unique sense of humor. When we checked into the conference site, we were given ID tags that said

"Hello my name is ____________"The blank was barely big enough for one name. Our airman wrote in small letters, "I am the Walrus, goo goo goo joob." (Apparently, he was a fan of John Lennon and the Beatles). Many of our fellows attending the conference were hearty Texans. I got a kick out of watching their approach to my friend. They would grab his hand and say, "Hello….." As they squinted to read the small words on my friend's lapel, they slowly concluded they were holding the hand of a lunatic. Without saying what they read, they slowly released his hand and backed away from him.

Participants at the conference included youth who spoke only Spanish, French, Italian and German. The program was all in English, so they all needed a translator. I learned that the designated Spanish translator couldn't attend. Tommy applied for the job first. Although he spoke fluent Spanish, like, he couldn't manage the job, so he suggested that I apply for the job. To my surprise, I was good at it.

Simultaneous translation requires that you listen to the speaker and then say it in another language on your microphone. While you are saying what you previously heard, the speaker has gone on to new words. You have to remember it to translate it while saying the previous thought of the speaker. It can be tricky. I was surprised that I could do it. My only problem was trying to translate a word that I wasn't familiar with in Spanish. The speaker said, "Judas was a fool." I couldn't remember the Spanish word for fool. (It was necio). I said in Spanish, "Judas was an idiot." Pretty close.

In one session, an American woman who had made illustrations for the Good News for Modern Man New Testament was showing her pictures and telling which verses they applied to. The illustrator had a musical kind of voice. I needed to use the bathroom. I told my listeners to get the verses from the pictures being flashed on the screen. I put my headset down and stepped out of my booth.

Almost immediately, an official from the conference grabbed me by the lapels. He asked, "What are you doing??" I was taken aback and said rather timidly, "Going to the bathroom. That's OK, isn't it?" The man let me go and moved on to the next booth.

It turned out that the Italian translator thought the woman was being condescending. Instead of translating her comments, he was telling his listeners jokes. They were funny jokes because Italians were laughing loudly. The man who accosted me didn't think the New Testament was particularly funny.

The keynote speaker of the Conference was Billy Graham. I got to translate his sermon into Spanish. Billy Graham had hit fame in his rallies about the time my parents left the US for the mission field. Billy Graham was an incredible preacher known around the world. He got to know politicians from both parties. He became close to Richard Nixon and later thought this was a mistake.

I had heard many sermons by Billy Graham, so translating for him was easy. I wanted to shake his hand, to tell him how much my father admired him, how my father and other missionaries imitated his preaching style. Unfortunately, Graham left before I could complete my work in the translation booth.

A Period Of Melancholy

1968 was the end of our five-year term, and we were returning to the US. I knew that an era was ending for me. I would still be my parents' son, but I would never be a Spain MK again. I didn't like the huge change in my life but didn't know what else to do but to follow my parents back to the US. I had vowed not to return to Mississippi, but I wasn't ready to make a clean break from my family. I had never worked a job and had not come close to supporting myself.

I had an idea: Mark Singer, Nikki Szulc, and other members of my graduating class had been accepted into the American University of Paris. I decided to try this too. I could continue my relationships, and the wonderful senior year I had just experienced would not end.

I was 17 years and six months, not quite an adult. I presented this to my parents, and they shot it down. They told me that the small scholarship the Mission Board provided would not come to me in a country outside the US. They reminded me that I didn't speak French. How would I pay for tuition? How would I eat? I told them I would find a way. Finally, they told me that they wouldn't allow it. I was in a state of rebellion, but I was practical enough to know they were right. As an obedient son, I accepted their decision and returned to the US to attend Mississippi College. I sulked for about a year.

Had I known the future, I would not have been upset. My friends who attended the Paris college ended up leaving after one semester, Mark to a college in Turkey and Nikki back to the US. My high school friendships receded into the past. I kept in contact with my friends, but they went their way, and I went mine.

This was a crucial moment for a third-culture kid like me. It almost always happened to a missionary kid returning to the US for college. We loved our country from afar, but when we reenter the country, we see the racism and xenophobia and want to leave.

As a third culture kid who spent four out of every five years outside the US, I considered what I claimed as my family. Besides my biological relatives, I had three other kinds of family: the first was the missionaries and their kids. These had been my friends for almost two decades. Second, I had a Spanish Baptist family. We had protected their churches and ability to worship during the worst days of persecution in the 1950s and through the mid-1960s. Missionary kids dove deep into Spanish culture, and the church members considered us to be their children, too. Third was the expatriate population in

Spain. We had a lot in common, and this made many of them my friends. I would lose all this when I went back to college. If I returned to Spain after I finished college, I would have to rebuild these relationships.

I enjoyed going to the movies in Spain. I could get around easily on public transportation. In the US, I would need a car and a driver's license. I enjoyed playing trumpet duets with Bruce Hickman (an MK whose parents worked for the Assemblies of God). We did specials at a variety of Protestant churches. Movies were more expensive in the US and required a car. Going back to the US for college would shrink my world dramatically.

I returned to the US for college because I needed to be close to the only family I felt I had left.

Returning To A Chaotic America In 1968

1968 was not a good year for a Third Culture Kid. The country was still reeling from the assassinations of Martin Luther King and Robert Kennedy. There had been riots in major cities after MLK's death. Many democrats felt unrepresented after the death of RFK. Demonstrations against the war in Vietnam and against young men being sent to Vietnam against their will led to demonstrations against the draft. Rather than going to Vietnam, many young men moved to Canada. Throughout my college years I considered this possibility.

My political views would be accepted by a majority of the population in Spain and by American expatriates there. Mississippians at the time were for the war and against the Civil Rights movement. I was a stranger in a strange land.

Mississippi College allowed one kind of hazing for freshman boys—shaving their heads. My father had suffered this in 1940 but had a lot less hair to lose than I did. Shaving a man's hair happened when you went into the military or into jail. This bothered me.

I went to the registration office to find my classes. An upperclassman named Ronnie Prevost shaved my beautiful hair. My hair would grow back, but long hair had been the symbol of young men of the time. I vowed revenge against Ronnie. Later, I learned that he had a glass eyeball. I decided to forgo revenge.

After I lost my hair, I went to the cafeteria for lunch. I sat down at a table with a group of freshman boys. It wasn't hard to find them. One of them was Jimmy Lewis, who became a friend of mine later. I didn't realize at the time that his aunt had been a missionary or that our families knew each other. We both agreed that we were "dumb clucks" for coming to this college.

As I lay in my dorm, I felt out of control. My hair was gone. I was subject to a much stricter set of rules than the college. They considered themselves substitute parents. What could I do to show resistance?

My first step was to grow a mustache. It came in before the hair on my head returned. It was a small act of defiance, but it meant something to my family. The last Whitten to have a mustache was my great-grandfather, Henry. A year later, I began to smoke cigarettes. I had been strongly against smoking. In 1964, my Uncle W.A. left a pack of cigarettes. I crushed it instead of giving it back, telling my sisters, "This has enough nicotine to kill a man if you chewed on it." My uncle never knew what happened to those cigarettes. It was a stupid decision on my part. I smoked until 1976 and was fortunate to quit when I did.

I had learned to play the trumpet in high school. I signed up for the college band. One day in practice, the leader told us to move the tune-up a fifth. A fellow trumpeter and friend of mine, Jack Land, told the bandleader, "David and I wouldn't know a fifth if it bit us on the leg." He was right, although I was embarrassed. If they had asked me what a fifth was, I would have said that I didn't drink alcoholic beverages.

The cost of attending college, including room and board, was about $1500 per semester. I had a $500 scholarship from the Foreign Mission Board, and MC gave $500 to each missionary kid. That left me with $500 to earn in four months, $125 per month at $1.25 per hour minimum wage. Around 20 hours a week would pay my tuition debt. More hours than that would buy me toiletries and pay for washing my clothes at a washateria. There was nothing left for entertainment, for a car, or for dating.

I got a job at the college cafeteria. Not having worked before, I didn't realize that it was a bad idea to excel at a job everybody hated. I was stuck for a while shoveling ice into drinks. The bucket for the ice was heavy, and nobody filled in for me when I walked down the line to refill it. I had no protection for my hands. When I placed the scoop into the ice, my hands would freeze. I would occasionally hit the other hand with the metal scoop. When my hands thawed out, I ached from the cold and from the bruise I had caused on my other hand when it was frozen.

I was still in my shy and bitter stage. I did not speak to many people working at the cafeteria. The non-students (other than management) were all Black. One day, an older Black woman asked me, "You hate Black?" I said, "No. I just don't understand a lot of what you are saying." She explained this to her co-workers, and they became more friendly to me.

Dorm Life

My high school graduation announcements got me around $150 in gifts. Since I couldn't afford a car, I spent most of it on a 19-inch TV console. It had a stereo radio and a record player. I began buying LPs. I joined Colombia Record Club, and for my monthly purchases got all the Bob Dylan recordings I could.

I was on the third floor of Chrestman dorm. It didn't have air conditioning. The top floor was freshmen men. The basement housed the football team. When I tried to practice my trumpet, I could hear shouts of "shut up" from the basement. My roommate was as shy as I was. We watched my TV set, ad commented on the shows or mocked the commercials. That was all the conversation we had. His friend group was very different than mine, so when he went to eat, I didn't go with him.

Freshmen boys in college can be strange. My neighbor one door down from me was Clark Olmstead, whom we nicknamed the "dynamic nudist." Clark did not wear clothes when relaxing in his room. If he wanted something from a neighbor, he would emerge from his room and knock on your door. Nerdy kids like me were sensitive to the "gay" card. If you were skinny, wore glasses and did not hang around with one girl, you were vulnerable to innuendos that you were homosexual. Simply looking at Clark's penis was enough to start the innuendos. When he came to the door, you had to look at the ceiling.

Clark brought a pet boa to his room. He would encourage you to pat his snake, knowing it would probably bite you. He thought this was very funny. Having a large snake in his room reduced the number of people who wanted to visit Clark. It also discouraged the floor monitor from going into his room when he was in class.

Clark kept his boa in a terrarium. During a cold spell, he placed a 40-watt bulb into the terrarium to keep his snake warm. He found the light kept him awake, so he placed a blanket over the terrarium. He woke to discover his snake had been baked to death. All the snake's scales fell off, and he swept them into a pile under my door. When I saw this, I swept the scales back to his room. RIP snake.

Another dorm mate taught me an unusual skill. He sat down, leaned back and used a cigarette light to light his own farts. I was thankful for him and for me that he was wearing pants. His butt looked like a small blowtorch. I didn't ask if his underwear had singe marks on them. A third dorm mate sent someone to ask me to come to his room. When I arrived, his door was shut and there were two guys by the door giggling. Long before the Big Brother show, I had learned to expect the unexpected. I didn't touch the doorknob. Another student twisted it open and got a burn on his wrist from electricity. That was the old "attach a live wire to your doorknob." I didn't appreciate it and was sorry for the guy who got burned.

In my freshman year, four MC students who were in a musical play burned to death in a car accident near the college. The one student who survived was gay. This was before coming out was safe. His classmates saw the signs in his behavior, and the college administration heard the rumors about him. They considered homosexuality an abomination of the Lord. They waited until he was one semester from graduating to expel him.

I knew nothing about homosexuality until I got to a Baptist college. I was assigned to a dorm during a summer semester that had the reputation of being a gay hangout. I had no quarrel with gay students, and I knew that I was straight. MC's discrimination against gay students was one of the reasons I didn't like MC.

Thirty years later, I taught a class on Multicultural issues. I asked my students to give a presentation titled "My Multicultural Self." A young woman proudly stated she was gay and mentioned that she had graduated from Mississippi College. After the class, I offered her my sympathies, assuming she had been closeted and miserable there. She told me that MC had been a great experience and that she had met a woman who was the love of her life there. I was glad for her.

Having told you how MC had changed for the better in the treatment of gay people, I have to take some of my praises back. I googled MC and Homosexuality and discovered that MC had petitioned for and gotten a waiver of Department of Education requirements that they treat gay people equally to straight people. They got the waiver under a federal law designed to allow you to discriminate if your religious beliefs required it.

My Efforts To Escape Mississippi

I kept in contact with some of my classmates from MHS. One was Lindsay Tunnell, who was enrolled in a college in Arizona. The school sounded interesting, so I applied. On spring break in 1969 I booked a flight from Mississippi to Arizona, from Arizona to Washington, D.C. and then back to Mississippi. I had gotten a student discount card. The whole trip cost about $150.

I hoped to be accepted by the college, and then to persuade them to give me enough financial aid that I could survive there. Arizona was interesting. I had a good time with Lindsay, but I was not accepted. In the interview, I was asked the last time I cried. I said it was when I learned that RFK had died. I was left wondering if they thought I cried too much or not enough.

A friend at Washington University if DC let me stay in a dorm for a couple of days. I had tried to set up a reunion for classmates in DC. Only Liz Visbeek showed up. She was disappointed at the turnout and left. Linda Collins let me stay one night at her house.

Her father made sure I was in the basement. The next day he dropped me off where he worked, at the Pentagon. I returned to Mississippi, resigned to the fact I would probably have to spend four years at MC.

Selling Dictionaries In Pennsylvania

I had no idea what I would do for the summer. One day I met a student who had signed on for a job with the Southwestern Corporation. They hired college students to sell their dictionaries and an encyclopedia. I was intrigued by the amount of money he said I could make. At 18 I was pretty naive when it came to offers of money. I signed on for the summer.

Four MC students signed to sell the books. One had a car. He drove us to Nashville, where we went through training. I learned how to canvass a neighborhood and finding houses that had school-aged children in them. The key was to find a talkative kid outside and to ask him about other kids in the neighborhood. I would get the names and ages of the kids and their grades in school if he knew it.

The most important part of the training was to get into someone's house to sell them. We were trained to ring the doorbell and then turn out back on the door. We didn't want them to think I was peering into their homes. When they answered the door, I would turn around and flash my best smile. I would say, "I am talking to parents who are interested in their kids' education. If they tried to say they were not interested, I would say, "That's what Mrs. Jones {next door neighbor} thought, but then she said that it was worth listening to. It didn't matter that Mrs. Jones hadn't actually said it. If the person at the door was undecided about inviting me in, I would put my head down and walk in place. I wasn't pushing my way in, but it looked like I expected to be admitted to their home. Usually, they let me in.

Once I was in the house, I asked them to bring their school children in because this involved them. I would ask the kids what they liked about school and what they found hardest about their classes. If they said "Math" I would pull out the book that had a summary of math at all levels and show how simple it was. I would ask the parents, "If this book could help your child improve at math, wouldn't it be worth $20?" Making the parents feel guilty was a very effective sales technique.

The dictionaries, one for elementary school and one for higher grades, were $10. If they agreed to buy the books, I told them I needed a $5 deposit. The books wouldn't arrive until the end of the summer. The $5 deposits paid my bills until I could collect them at the end of the summer.

My friends and I had been assigned to Ebensburg, Pennsylvania. It was a small blue-collar town in a hilly part of central Pennsylvania. I enjoyed the camaraderie with them. In the afternoon, we would eat a bar that made pizzas in an old oven. I was barely 18 and still had qualms about drinking beer.

My mother knew that I was lonely. She sent me a letter every day! I bought a bicycle. It increased the number of people I could make my sales pitch to every day. I would right up and down hills, and I had a sensation of being free.

Halfway through the summer, I had a crisis of conscience. I was telling poorly educated parents from the hills that my books would improve their kids' performance when it was often clear to me that the children had learning disabilities that were not improved by the book by itself. I began to doubt my speech.

My daily schedule usually involved making as many presentations as possible and then waiting for my friends to pick me up in their car sometime around 5 P.M. Waiting under a tree, I began to examine my anger at my parents. They hadn't let me have my way, but they were rights. Why was I angry at them? They were the best parents I knew. I was being an ungrateful jerk. I decided to return to Mississippi to make my apologies, a sort of prodigal son moment.

I took a 14-hour bus trip from Ebensburg, Pennsylvania, to Clinton. My parents were pleased to see my change of disposition. When I tried to apologize, they brushed it off, saying they had forgiven me long ago. I had only a couple weeks with them until they had to fly to New York to board an ocean liner back to Spain. A church had given them a generous "love offering," and they shared it with me.

We flew to New York, staying a night at the Taft Hotel, just as we had done in other furloughs. We talked about old times and how we would miss each other. We took a taxi to the ship, and I boarded it with them. When we heard the announcement, "All ashore that's going ashore," I got off. It was a difficult time for all of us. The passengers were given streamers to throw to people saying goodbye to them. After a few failures, I caught a streamer. It broke as the ship moved away from the wharf. I was alone in New York City.

I had a bright spot. I had a ticket to the popular musical "Hair." It was an edgy musical, with most of the cast stripping naked at the intermission. A fake cop said, "You're all under arrest for coming to this nasty communist show!" I enjoyed it thoroughly and had something to brag about when I got back to Mississippi College.

I needed a place to stay. The Taft Hotel was well out of my range. I ended up getting a $5 room in a seedy hotel off Times Square. When I settled in, I found a pornographic magazine. I put it back in the dresser and pushed the dresser against the door. There were a lot of weird noises during the night, and I didn't get much sleep.

The next day, I went to the bus station to get a ticket to Ebensburg. The station was full of young people, hippies, college students and the group we called "freaks." There were so many of them that some of them were sitting on the floor. Where were they going? To quote Joni Mitchell, "going down to Yasgur's farm, going to join in a rock and roll band." They were headed to the small rural town of Woodstock, New York.

I had heard of the Woodstock festival on TV. The admission was $40. I never asked what the bus to Woodstock would cost. I had enough money to make it back to Ebensburg. I believed my landlord would let me stay without paying until two weeks later when I would distribute books and collect the remainder of what people owed.

I bought my ticket and returned to Ebensburg. I learned later that the number of people at the festival turned out to be 10 times what they expected. They stopped charging. People shared food and sleeping bags. It would be a wonderful experience for me. Unfortunately, it was not me. If I had a friend to go with, I would have tried it. I was too scared to go alone.

I saw the moon landing at my landlord's house. When my money ran out, I cut grass and did whatever I could to make money. I distributed the books and rode with my friends to Nashville. Most of what I had collected I owed to the company. The man handing me a check shook his head in disappointment. I was not ashamed. I had reconciled with my parents and had enough money for my textbooks at MC. I had also learned life-changing lessons. I was beginning to build confidence in my abilities.

STUCK AT MC FOR A 2ND YEAR

When I left for the summer job, I had failed to reserve a room for myself in a dorm. This meant that I had to be assigned a room with another roommate I didn't know. My room was in Ratliff Hall, an older dorm that my dad had once lived in. My roommate was a transfer student. He liked my having a TV. He and his friends would come to our room on Sundays to watch NFL football.

My roommate's favorite adverb was the F word or F##ing. If he was trying to remember something, he would say, "The F##ing, the F##ing, the F##ing…." He was a stuck record, repeating the word for copulation. It was new to me.

I was still hostile to the college. I changed my job to the library. That was more of my style. The minimum was $1.45 per hour.

Tuition hadn't gone up.

I had made a friend named Wayne Grey. His mother was a devout Baptist and had met my mother. He was a bit more worldly than her at the time. I visited his home once. He took me and others out to a wooded lot to smoke pot. It was an incredible experience. I liked it, but didn't have the enthusiasm then to try it again. This was an era where possession of Marijuana in Texas could get you 30 years in jail. My motto was to not do anything that can alter your life for the worst.

Wayne and another friend, Jim Smith, had cars. He had heard of a job available at McDonalds. We all applied and were hired. I ended up at the French fry machine. McDonalds had a vat with boiling oil. You lowered a tray of precut fries into it, set an alarm, and then removed the fries when the alarm went off. A delay in removing the fries could result in all the fires burning.

One of the two listed above decided it was funny to turn my alarm off. I had other jobs besides watching my fries cook. When I didn't hear the alarm, my fries burned. The offender was walking away from me, giggling. I aimed a powerful kick at his butt and missed by inches. Thankfully! Fighting would have probably got us both fired.

I was employed at McDonalds before the food chain hit it big. Our store had an enclosed area by the cash registers. To the side of this was concrete tables that could probably accommodate eight people total. McDonalds didn't anticipate that people would eat the food at the store. They actively discouraged kids from hanging around the store. Things changed dramatically!

KILLINGS AT JACKSON STATE

The major college in the area was an HBCU called Jackson State. They didn't discourage white people from enrolling. They existed because the white colleges in Mississippi had forbidden Black people from attending these state-run schools.

Demonstrations against the war in Vietnam had increased exponentially in the early 1970s. Governors became concerned at this escalation and began calling up the state National Guard to put down the demonstrations. In the spring of 1970, the National Guard at Kent State University in Ohio fired live ammunition at demonstrators who were a comfortable distance from them, killing four students. This caused an enormous nationwide reaction.

Demonstrations against racial discrimination in Mississippi had been continuous since the early 1960s. Demonstrations against the war added to the fervor of those involved. A disproportionate percentage of American soldiers in Vietnam were Black.

Someone set fire to a garbage truck. The firemen who sought to put out the fire got backup from city and state policemen. At one point, 50 policemen opened fire on a dormitory, shattering all the windows. Two unarmed young men were killed.

The public response took a page from the early days of civil rights conflict. They said the conflict was caused by outside agitators. They claimed to be shooting back at a sharpshooter, although no evidence of one was found. The victims became non-persons. They were to blame, not the policemen who opened fire on unarmed kids.

I was beyond outraged. College students had been murdered ten miles from me. The victims were both Black. There would be no consequences for the perpetrators' acts, just as there were no consequences for years against white shooters who killed Black people. I felt like I was living in a madhouse.

I wrote to my parents about my feelings. They agreed with me but were more concerned about my emotional state. My mother asked a good friend of hers to talk to me. This woman made the mistake of saying the news reports were wrong, creations of outside agitators. I told her that I wouldn't accept that propaganda and asked her to leave.

A Summer Back In Spain

The mission board gave each MK one free trip home to their parents during their four years in the US. I decided that the summer after my sophomore year, 1970, would be a good time to go.

Helen and I took our cousin Judy with us to Spain. As an avid fan of the Tonight Show with Johnny Carson, I had gotten three tickets for the night we were to stay in New York City. There were now direct flights to Europe from New York. My parents didn't get a week-long vacation on an ocean liner.

After we arrived in New York, I discovered that the Tonight Show was only for people over 18. Johnny was well known for his double entendres. I didn't think Judy would get those jokes at 15 years old, but we had to leave her in the hotel room while we went to the show.

Johnny Carson had Tony Randall and Jack Klugman on the show, talking about their new series, The Odd Couple. It turned out to be a great show. I marveled that the audience for the show was in a room smaller than the auditorium of my high school.

With Helen and me gone from the house, my parents had rented an apartment near the Plaza Castilla, which was a starting point for buses that would take you anywhere in town. It also had a subway entrance that would do the same for you.

The Whitten family had a cat named Bilbo Baggins, named for a character in a book John enjoyed. My parents' apartment was on the third floor. The apartments had a skylight that connected all the apartments with a clothesline. Bilbo Baggins got used to climbing out a window on one corner and jumping to an open window perpendicular to him. One day, my mother had locked one of the windows. When Bilbo tried the jump, he had little to cling to and fell down three stories. Margaret ran downstairs to collect what she thought would have been his lifeless corpse. He had hit every clothesline on his way down, breaking the fall. He had a dislocated hip but was otherwise OK.

I visited the base and saw some of my former teachers. I ran into Colleen Fahey and learned from her that one of my teachers had propositioned her. My memories of high school were tarnished a little.

In spite of this, I considered the possibility of getting a teaching degree and returning to the base as an English teacher. It was not a slam dunk. I would have to apply from the US and hope I would be assigned to the base in Madrid. The money was good, but I had deeper concerns. I had met former students of MHS when I was a student and thought they were a little pathetic in their desire to continue their own internal legend of high school. I would later find out similar examples at MHS. If "You cannot go home again" was true, it was also equally true that you couldn't go back to high school after you graduated. I wanted to soar from college, not cower in the past.

I was glad to be back in Spain, although in my two years of absence, Spain had changed dramatically. There were more cars, more money for people who had been poor, and a more confident attitude in the population.

I concluded that I would always identify with Spain, but I couldn't be Spanish. Even if my diction were perfect, it would always be clear to any Spanish person I met that I was an "Americano."

We visited Barcelona and saw our old friends. We stopped at Denia and hung out a little with Jorge Pastor. Then, it was time to go back to college.

Cousin Judy had gone back to the US before Helen and me. We decided to spend a couple of days in London. My parents had gone to Baptist conferences there but hadn't taken me. I had been a Francophile since third grade. There was so much to see.

We visited the Tower of London. We saw Westminster Abbey and saw the Tower of Big Ben. (I'm beginning to recite lyrics to Roger Miller's song "England Swings.") I had enjoyed a course in English literature and was awed to find so many of the great English poets buried in Westminster Abbey's Poet's Corner.

Our big decision came when we had to make a choice. Would we visit the theater where Shakespeare had put on his great plays, in a town called Stratford-on-Avon, or would we go to Wembley Stadium, a huge soccer stadium in London, to attend a rock concert with Crosby, Stills & Nash, Three Dog Night, and other of our favorite rock groups? I should have chosen the English literature alternative. I had missed Woodstock, and I didn't want to miss this opportunity. We spent six hours listening to great rock and roll.

I returned to Mississippi College for a dorm room I had reserved. My new roommate, Paul Taylor, was a friend. His father was a professor at the Baptist seminary in New Orleans. He had been adopted out of Sellers Orphanage in New Orleans. He didn't want to talk about it.

My Junior Year Has Its Ups And Downs

I had left MC in a more organized way than I had left my freshman year. Not only was I in a room of my choosing, but I had friends in rooms near me. This was going to be a great year for us.

While in Spain during the summer, I had taken stock of my future. I would graduate from college with a philosophy major. What could I do with that major other than teach or be a bum? I decided to expand my studies. I already had 12 hours of English. Three more English classes would give me a second major. 18 hours in education would prepare me to get a certificate to teach High School English. It was an occupation. I had thought of being an English teacher since the three English classes I took with Mr. Morris in high school.

Computer enrollment in schools was in its infancy in 1970. Students didn't have access to computer screens. MC didn't have an email address or an account. It did have a computer that filled up almost an entire floor in a college building. In order to enroll, students went from table to table in an outdoor enrolling session. Each class had enough computer cards for its capacity. Once you gathered computer cards for your classes, you turned them in, and that was your semester schedule.

Many people needed a class that was offered once a year. When collecting your cards, you go in those lines first. It was August, and everyone was perspiring heavily and in a grumpy mood.

KEN SPELL

As I waited in line, I heard a commotion coming from a student I didn't recognize. The noise came from a tall young man with black hair. He was wearing a black trench coat in spite of the heat. He looked like "The Shadow," a character from horror movies. Think (in a creepy voice), "Who knows what evil lurks in the hearts of men? The Shadow does." It was Ken Spell, a transfer from Hinds Junior College. He was spouting out famous quotes and references from science fiction novels. Most people thought he was crazy. I liked him immediately.

The spell came from Vicksburg, Mississippi. The siege of Vicksburg was from before he was born, but its memory seemed baked into the DNA of people from Vicksburg. Years later, when I moved to southeast Pennsylvania, I invited Ken to visit me for a tour of the Gettysburg battlefield. The North had won both battles on July 4, 1863. He shuddered and declined my invitation. He disliked rednecks and racists as much as I did, but he carried the same pain Southern white Americans have carried from past history.

Spell had a strict, domineering mother. She had allowed Ken to attend Hinds Junior College in Jackson, the first time he was out of her control. Spell gravitated to the hippies at Hinds. He made friends with people who took drugs and embraced the counterculture. He made one female friend, his first female friend ever. She had sex with him once. More on that later.

When Ken's mother learned about his hippie friends, she transferred him at the end of junior college to Mississippi College. She reasoned that a Baptist college would bring Ken under control. She was wrong.

Spell fell into our social group. This included Paul Taylor, my roommate, whom we called the Mad Monk; Ken Nail, who was Tio Taco, and a timid young man whose name I forget. He was convinced that his mother was spying on him, using a policeman who was notorious for appearing at incidents where police abused Black people. We called him the Freak. My nickname was Faustus. I wasn't fond of the name. Spell didn't have a nickname.

We pronounced his name with a heavy German accent, "Herr Schpell". We had other students who were in the group, but not enough to get a nickname. They included Jim Smith and Wayne Grey.

We weren't a bad influence on Ken. We played cards in our rooms and watched programs on my TV set. After we finished watching Johnny Carson at midnight, we would go out to have a snack at midnight diner. Ken loved it. As a loner in high school, he was happy to have friends.

I played a couple of pranks on Ken. In December, just before Christmas break, Ken brought a new solo album by John Lennon. We listened to the songs on it, and then Ken left it to me in my room as he went to a class. While he was gone, I switched John Lennon for a Lawrence Welk album I had. (I have no idea why I had it!). When Ken returned, I gave him the LP. Fortunately for his sanity that Christmas, he discovered the switch and got the original album back. I am sure his parents would have liked Lawrence Welk more than he would have.

That Christmas, I decided on another prank. I had noticed that some ignorant people didn't know the difference between Stokely Carmichael, the Black nationalist, and Hoagy Carmichael, the musician who wrote "Stardust" and "Georgia on My Mind. I took Papaw's upright typewriter and wrote a fictional letter to Spell from the "Kosciusko Klan." I filled it with outrageous misspellings and accused Spell of being a follower of Hoagy Carmichael. I warned Spell to watch his butt. I put a stamp on it and got someone to mail the letter from Kosciusko.

When Spell got the letter, he was scared and honored. Nobody wants to be threatened by a terrorist group. He was honored that somebody had noticed him! Spell's parents weren't honored. They got in touch with the FBI. I imagine my letter is in a warehouse. The statute of limitations ran out on that more than 50 years ago.

I doubt Spell's parents ever learned the truth about the letter. His mother had met my mother at a speech my mother made. Having me as one of his friends led his mother to worry less about him. Ken would be my friend for more than 50 years until his untimely death.

When Spell returned to college in January, he stuck his head into my room, asking if I knew about the Kosciusko Klan. I hadn't prepared for this. The smile on my face made him realize I wrote the letter.

Ken was a voracious reader. He had more books than me. He collected so many books in his life that he had to donate them in order to get around in his apartment. He gave me funny and interesting books for a long time. I wasn't the only beneficiary of his gifts. He bought books that other friends he had from college and his sister's children would like. He donated enough for a small city library.

Ken loved reading science fiction, books from the Greatest Books list, and political books. Unfortunately, these books were not required reading in his classes. He rebelled against being required to read anything he didn't want to. That made it more difficult for him to pass his classes. I looked at his grades and estimated that if he didn't get one good grade, he would be denied a return to MC.

I had him enroll in a philosophy class. It was taught by my major professor, Dr. Joe Cooper. I knew what Dr. Cooper asked on his tests. Dr. Cooper, like most professors, was more enthusiastic about matters that he would test on. I took copious notes, using red and yellow markers to highlight what Dr. Cooper thought was the most important. At the end of the semester, I called all the students I was helping to discuss the final exam. Repeating these facts to my group helped me to remember them on the test. In the midst of our study session, I looked at Spell. He was sleeping.

After Spell flunked out of college, he moved in with his parents at their Vicksburg home. His dad had a lifelong job with a railroad company. Spell turned that option down. He got tired of being with his parents and eventually moved to California. He had come out of the closet, and California was a welcoming place for him.

Over the years, I visited with Spell at Mamaw and Papaw's house. He visited me in Jamaica when I was in the Peace Corps. He visited me in San Francisco when I went to a graduate conference there. In all those times, he remained shy, funny, and a picky eater. I invited him to join me at my 50th anniversary of graduating from MC. He was going to come, but months before our reunion died of an embolism. He was my most faithful friend.

Spell spent years writing a novel about his years at Hinds Junior College with friends like Gargoyle and the only female friend he ever had, whose name was Bobbye. He worked me in as a character named "Julian." He would send me pages to comment on. Ideally, the book should have ended in 1971, with the hero (him) shaking the dust off his feet as he left college for bigger and better things. Unfortunately, he was as uncertain about the conclusion of his book as he had been about his own career.

The book was unfinished when he died.

More On My Junior Year

My friend, Jimmy Lewis, had been given the job as editor of the student newspaper, the Collegian. I asked him if I could write a political column. Jimmy knew that I was on the opposite end of the political spectrum from him. He wanted variety in the paper. Ken Nail was given the job of reporting on-campus sports. Other mutual friends of Jimmy and me were on the paper with me, including Catherine Chappell, who later became Jimmy's wife. My father and Catherine's father had been classmates at MC.

My columns were pretty much unread by students, most of whom cared very little for politics. They got the attention of the president of the college, Lewis Noble, and the dean of students, Charles Scott. We had some controversies that got us viewership.

Jimmy learned that the employees of Campus Security had a gun with a few bullets. Ours was a quiet campus, with no need for the officer to pull a gun on anybody. The Collegian reported the existence of a deadly weapon on our campus. In retrospect, it seems like such an innocent time that Jimmy would be alarmed at having a gun in the hands of poorly prepared campus cops who were not certified as peace officers. Nothing came of this.

Stokely Carmichael came to town, speaking at the HBCU institution, Jackson State. Jimmy, Ken Nail, Ken Spell, and I attended. It was like a scene from the movie Animal House in which a group of white students find themselves the only white people in a large crowd of suspicious Black people.

Carmichael, a Black separatist. His message to Black people was that if they wanted to get power, they should buy land in an African country. The MC students were very quiet. At one point, an inebriated Black man began heckling Stokely. The crow murmured at the interruptions. Stokely asked the crow to give some understanding because the man had a disease. When the heckler didn't stop, Stokely said, "We will have to educate this man. If we can't, we will have to kill him." This led to menacing gestures toward the white kids. We slumped down so far in our chairs that those in the back would have thought our chairs were unoccupied.

Another racial controversy involved the so-called "Republic of New Africa," which was to be less than 20 miles from MC. This group didn't want to relocate to Africa. They wanted Black separatists to buy up land and then declare themselves independent from the United States.

The land was purchased, and the leaders had a press conference announcing their intentions. The separatist group gathered on a plot of land in the country to enjoy the beginning of their new country. The governor, attorney general, and any government official close to a microphone threatened the use of the National Guard and even the military.

Anybody who was not grandstanding knew the New Republic did not have a chance. The day after the press conference, Jimmy asked if any members of his staff wanted to interview the leaders. Spell and I volunteered. We visited the site of the Republic and found nothing there but KFC boxes, empty beers, and cigarette stubs. At a Stop and Go store, we asked a middle aged lady running it what she had heard. It had not affected her sleep. She turned to a young Black man working for her and asked him what he knew. He gave the classic response of a man who worried about his job, "I don't know anything about anything."

My Dorm Room's Placement Led Me To Trouble

Paul and I were to have a corner room, the first room you approached as you entered the dorm. The room had two windows, one facing the dorm next to ours and one facing the main street. The windows were very low, giving people who walked by a very good view of our room if we didn't lower the curtains. The privacy issue didn't bother us as much as the concern for possible pranks. It was not unusual for someone to throw a bucket of water through a first-story window. We switched to a room at the back of the dorm, next to the showers.

That had its negatives too. People who were disgruntled in the floor above would stop it the drains for the shower to descend in a broom closet down to our floor, where it sometimes went into our room. We maintained towels ready to prevent this.

When we moved, I forgot to return my key. One of the students who took our place had a skeleton key. The two students were horticulture enthusiasts. Actually, they just grew marijuana plans.

Everyone in the dorm knew about their plants except for the floor monitor. The students were worried their room would be inspected when they were gone, so they moved their plants to my room. I didn't have a key for all the rooms, but I had a key to their room. Paul and I returned the plants to their room with a "No thank you" note.

Our new room was perfect for one forbidden activity, to allow a girl to climb in the back window. Paul had a skinny blonde as his first girlfriend. They hooked up, not in my room but in any place on campus where they had privacy. They got a special thrill in having her climb in the window to my room. I would return to find Linda (I think that was her name) standing in the room smiling. I didn't care about her being there and did not have any intention of telling on her.

The bottom dropped out when an anonymous student told on them. They were both called into the Dean of Students and expelled. In an effort to prevent this, Paul and Linda said it was no big deal. Everybody knew, and Ken Nail and I could testify that they were not having sex there.

That didn't save them. Ken and I were called before Dean Scott to face accusations that we had known of violations of the rule and hadn't told on them. We both said it was true. We didn't invite her in and urged her to get out once we discovered what was going on.

Ken and I were put on disciplinary probation for our senior years. I was forbidden to write for the Collegian. Ken transferred to Ole Miss and graduated from there. I stayed at MC and didn't have a roommate for the rest of my studies at MC. I got a room to myself for free,

In my meeting with Dean Scott, he informed me that he and Dr. Nobles knew I was a communist. I should have asked him what beliefs I had that identified me as a communist. I found him creepy and threatening, so I ended the conversation as quickly as I could. I managed to stay out of trouble and, in my senior year, had my probation lifted.

Paul and Linda never enrolled in another college. I felt that was a tragedy. Other colleges would have taken them, but they didn't try. 20 years later, Paul died in an auto accident in Memphis.

Making Garbage Bags At A Plastic Factory

In early 1971, I learned of a job at a plastic factory in rural Clinton. The factory melted plastic chips in an oven and then blew the plastic upward, where it made a thin layer of plastic that was fed through a series of pulleys. The machine-made perforations to divide the plastic into bags. The inner workings of the factory were beyond. That is why I only made $.25 more than minimum wage. Men our age who didn't go to college ran the machines and got $.50 more than minimum wage. They knew when to cut the bubble of plastic bags to end an order and then fix the plastic on the pulleys to start a new order.

My job was to bring bags of plastic pellets in to be poured into the furnace. The bags came from Arizona and sometimes had poisonous spiders in them. The bags were piled up outside, sometimes on a colony of fire ants. I got bitten a couple of times before I became good at avoiding these monsters. The permanent employees thought it was funny when I came into the workplace without a bag, yelling about fire ants.

My work at the plastic factory made me more sensitive to a generation of blue-collar young men who were not attending college. I didn't see them as any different from my college friends. When my co-worker brought me back to my dorm, I asked him to come in and meet my friends. He assumed that college students were much smarter than him, and he would be embarrassed by his ignorance. I assured him that my college friends were no different from anyone else. They drank beer and lied about their relationships with girls, like my blue-collar friend. (I didn't know this to be true, but it didn't seem like a stretch.). He never came into my dorm.

COMPLETING MY COLLEGE CAREER

Being kicked off the student newspaper reduced my social life considerably. During my senior year, I asked one coed out. She said no. I had developed the nerve to ask because I now had a car!

In the summer of 1971, Helen had graduated from college and had become engaged to be married. In our small community, those who knew the potential groom were not impressed. This included the mother of the groom.

My mother got emergency calls from her friends in Clinton telling her to come back and break up this disastrous wedding. By the time my mother was on her way back, Helen had already decided to back out of the wedding.

My mother spent time with the Mitchells and asked me what I needed most in college. I told her about a car. We looked for cars and found a 10-year-old Mercedes for $600. She paid half, and I got a loan for half. I loved my Mercedes and was thrilled that I could make a spontaneous visit to my grandparents' house any weekend. I no longer felt powerless.

I enrolled in summer school for the 1971 summer. This enabled me to take some education classes. My work at the library and at the plastic factory paid for the additional classes. The Mission Board did not have any scholarships for summer school.

In early 1972, as I approached graduation, I took a class in student teaching. I worked for an English teacher at a high school that had a sudden influx of Black students. 17 years after Brown vs. Board of Education had ordered schools to integrate with "all deliberate speed," courts decided that schools that were not allowing any Black students in had to speed it up. Students were assigned to schools out of their district, sometimes going by bus. It was an uneasy time for all the students. Many white parents pulled their children out of public schools and enrolled them in private schools that didn't admit Black students. Where Black and white kids went to the same school, there was little interaction between the groups. I got along with Black and white students. I noted that the only Black students who were accepted by white students who excelled at sports.

In the spring of 1972, we had a campaign for president of the student body. The two major candidates were Jack, an acquaintance of mine who came from Eupora, not far from my grandparents, and Jerry McBride, a social lion. The previous year, the president was Gayle Long, active in the Republican club at MC. We thought he had not done a very good job.

Jimmy Lewis, Catherine Chappell, and I decided to run a write-in candidate, someone who was not a student but who was well-known to everybody: Mickey Mouse.

Mickey in all his glory

We didn't have a large rodent to give a speech in the campaign. Mickey was in his 80s. He couldn't accept the job if he won because he wasn't actually a real person, and he wasn't a student.

We prepared a campaign platform, Mickey. The planks included:

Racial integration. He was the only black candidate.

His family was very familiar with the cafeteria. He objected to attempts to kill them all.

He was a contemporary of Mousie Tongue. This was a play on the name of the dictator of Communist China.

The previous occupant of the job had brought a mediocre rock band called "Mouse and the Boys."

Although Mickey appreciated giving his extended family some work, he thought he could do better.

It was all in good fun. Gayle Long was not amused. She later forgave us. She has been married to Roger Wicker the current senior US senator in Mississippi.

We watched in amusement as Jack and Jerry tried to figure out how to handle our candidate. Jack decided to ignore him. Jerry approached the microphone and announced, "I am Mickey Mouse!" The use of Mickey Mouse as an adjective usually means silly and inconsequential. Jerry certainly met this criterion. We laughed a lot. Jerry won the election by a landslide, leaving you to wonder if the students wanted a candidate who was silly and inconsequential or if they thought Jimmy, Catherine and I were being silly and inconsequential. It was a little of both.

The Two Most Important Parts Of My Senior Year

I graduated with a double major and a Mississippi license to teach English in a high school. This was OK, but it wasn't in my top two events.

I had feared being drafted from the moment I arrived in Mississippi in 1968. There was a lot of controversy around the draft for the military. I called it the "Selective Slavery System," not the "Selective Service System." It drafted a greater proportion of Black men than white men. This caused demonstrations accusing the government of having a system to get rid of Black men. In 1971, they introduced a lottery to assign priorities for being drafted by your date of birth. You were in the lottery after you turned 18. I had an exemption as a college student. It ended on my graduation in 1972. My lottery number was 45. I calculated I would be called up to serve in July.

I had pondered how I would apply as a conscientious objector. The CO status began in World War I and continued through World War II and the Korean conflict. It was never popular. COs in both of the major wars were jailed for resistance to the draft. My major problem was that the requirements to obtain the exemption required that I be a member of a religious group that forbade its members to serve. Baptists did not object to fighting in war, to killing other people in war.

Enter Mohammed Ali, the boxing champion. After winning the championship first time in 1964, he changed his name from Cassius Clay and announced he was a Muslim, a member of a Black sect. That did not sit well with a lot of Americans.

The military had a tradition of drafting celebrity young men and then giving them a cushy way to avoid actual military service. Ali could have done some exhibition fights for the entertainment of the troops. He could have fought real fights and made a lot of money. Ali considered himself a minister in the Muslim church. He refused to be drafted and was charged with the crime of resisting the draft. Ali was sensitive to racial injustices he had experienced as a youth in Louisville, Kentucky. He said, "No Vietcong ever called me nigger." (The Vietcong were the enemy in Vietnam.)

Ali was convicted and not allowed to box for money. His appeals went on for years. He was appealing to his draft board's refusal to accept him as a Muslim minister, which he said was due to the color of his skin.

In 1972, the US Supreme Court ruled that Mohammed Ali should have been accepted as a conscientious objector. This caused a lot of consternation at the draft board in Jackson, Mississippi. The director of the draft showed that if the Vietcong wouldn't use the N-word for Ali, he had no qualms doing so. He said that if that "N" was a conscientious objector, anybody who filed the claim would be approved.

I strenuously objected to the racial epithets being thrown around by the draft board but saw this as my opportunity! I filed for consideration as a conscientious objector. There was no way I would ever take up a gun against a fellow human. My major professor, Dr. Joe Cooper, accompanied me to the hearing. He told the examiners that he had known me for years and concluded that my objections to service qualified me as a CO. I was approved.

I Am Approved For The Peace Corps

I had been interested in the Peace Corps from its inception in 1962. Before I was approved as a conscientious objector, I had applied to the Peace Corps. In my application, I emphasized my experience in Spanish culture and my skills in the Spanish language. I assumed that I would be assigned to any country that accepted Peace Corps volunteers from the US border to the Tierra del Fuego in Argentina, except for Brazil. It was the only country that didn't speak Spanish.

I was very pleased to be accepted and offered a volunteer job in Nepal! The job was teaching science in a mountain village. There was no electricity and no running water. I would wash my body in a mountain stream. It sounded awfully cold. I had taken one science class in college, biology, and had made a D in it.

I wrote them back, declining the offer. I reminded them that if they assigned me to a Spanish-speaking country, they would not have to teach me Spanish. I would not need any cross-cultural training. Several weeks later, I got an offer to work in Guidance in Jamaica. The letter said that Spanish had been spoken in Jamaica. It had been, but not for 250 years. I didn't want to be written off as too picky, so I accepted the offer.

I had decided to leave the US when I graduated from college. Going into the Peace Corps would make this easier. Having a job in Jamaica would count as an alternate service. If you weren't going to serve in the military, you had to do some work in the public interest. The Peace Corps qualified.

Going Out On My Own

With a diploma and a job in Jamaica, which counted as public service, things were looking up. I was supposed to report to the training site in Washington, D.C., just before Independence Day. What was I to do in the meantime? Go to Spain, of course.

I boarded a flight to New York. It arrived late, giving me a layover for a night in a New York suburban hotel. When my parents got word that I would arrive late, in came from Jamaica. Jamaica, New York.

My brother, John was the only one of the original four kids still home. He missed the camaraderie we had when our family was six people. As the remaining bird in the nest with parents who worked outside the home, he was lonely. The Mission board was no longer paying the tuition for the school at Torrejon. He attended private schools in Madrid. When he graduated from High school, he was the only member of his graduation class.

That made him the valedictorian.

I had a month in Spain to have reunions with friends and my parents. I spent the month enjoying old family traditions and pondering my future. Leaving Spain in 1968 had been painful. I loved my life in Spain and all my friends there. When I left Spain in 1972, I had the feeling this would be a more permanent separation.

If I had something meaningful for me in Spain, I would have stayed; if there was a job with a future there, and indeed a future for me there, I would have stayed. If I stayed in Spain I would still be dependent on my parents, a bird that didn't leave the nest. The Peace Corps and Jamaica offered me hope and a future. I didn't know what that future would be, but I was ready for it.

I said goodbye to my missionary Aunts and Uncles, and my family. My father drove me to the airport in Valencia.

On July 1 1972, I took a ten-hour flight from Valencia to Madrid and from Madrid to New York. I watched a movie on the flight and listened to music on my headphones. I thought about my future.

Jamaica And The Peace Corps

I didn't see any grand design for my life. As a Christian I had been taught that God had a unique plan for everybody's life. If you reject the plan, you are miserable. If you follow it, you face a life of adventure and achievement. My parents were examples of this. **I had not received any plan yet from God.** Maybe I wasn't listening. Maybe I was following the plan but didn't know it.

I had little idea what my job in Jamaica would be like. I had little training in guidance and counseling. The people running the training program would have to bring me up to speed. I hadn't read much about Jamaica, but it had a contrast of nice tourist spots and poverty. I believed I could help with their needs.

Most of my questions were unanswerable. I fell asleep thinking it was not good to obsess on the unknown. Whatever my job was, I was determined to love it.

I had no idea the blessings God had in store for me. It was great to be an adult finally.

Made in the USA
Monee, IL
03 August 2025

22473151R00089